BETWEEN
LIVES

"This wide-ranging book gives an excellent overview of key areas of research in the further reaches of consciousness studies. Drawing on their own experience as well as a number of other sources, the authors articulate their inspiring vision for the transition to a higher frequency of consciousness, enabling the co-creation of a New Earth permeated with soul connection and awareness. They make it clear that this is the evolutionary trajectory of the Earth and that we would do well to tune into and embrace the process that is based on a fundamental oneness and interconnectedness."

DAVID LORIMER, MA, PGCE, FRSA, PROGRAM DIRECTOR
OF THE SCIENTIFIC AND MEDICAL NETWORK
AND EDITOR OF *PARADIGM EXPLORER*

"I agree with the authors' approach and conclusions and wish their book great success. Many people should read it."

PIM VAN LOMMEL, M.D., AUTHOR OF *CONSCIOUSNESS BEYOND LIFE*

"Andy Tomlinson and Reena Kumarasingham have choreographed a comprehensive, scholarly, spiritual self-help manual anyone can absorb to illuminate the breadth of soul consciousness. As a licensed psychologist and fellow Between Lives practitioner, I agree that we are all incarnate souls with the opportunity to elevate humanity."

LINDA BACKMAN, EDD, PSYCHOLOGIST, REGRESSION THERAPIST,
AND AUTHOR OF *BRINGING YOUR SOUL TO LIGHT*,
THE EVOLVING SOUL, SOULS ON EARTH, AND *SOUL DESIGN*

"This comprehensive overview of consciousness offers simple exercises and valuable tools to help raise your vibration to resonate with the light of Oneness in the New Consciousness that is now helping to create the New Earth."

PETER WRIGHT, CPLT, CHT, LBLT

"I love all the stories and examples of past life and in-between life experiences in *Between Lives*. The book offers very real evidence of the great scheme of things in our universe. The stories and examples included make the book relatable and accessible, providing readers with concrete evidence of the potential benefits of exploring the between-lives experience. The examples serve as both a means of illustrating the book's spiritual concepts and as proof that this exploration is a real and transformative process. A must-have book in your spiritual library."

DIANA COOPER, TEACHER, INTERNATIONAL SPEAKER, AND AUTHOR OF MORE THAN 30 BOOKS, INCLUDING *ANGELS OF LIGHT CARDS* AND *THE 36 SPIRITUAL LAWS THAT GOVERN ALL LIFE*

BETWEEN LIVES

Past-Life Regression,
Near-Death Experiences,
and the
Evolution of Consciousness

A Sacred Planet Book

ANDY TOMLINSON AND
REENA KUMARASINGHAM

Destiny Books
Rochester, Vermont

One Park Street
Rochester, Vermont 05767
www.DestinyBooks.com

Destiny Books is a division of Inner Traditions International

Sacred Planet Books are curated by Richard Grossinger, Inner Traditions editorial board member and cofounder and former publisher of North Atlantic Books. The Sacred Planet collection, published under the umbrella of the Inner Traditions family of imprints, includes works on the themes of consciousness, cosmology, alternative medicine, dreams, climate, permaculture, alchemy, shamanic studies, oracles, astrology, crystals, hyperobjects, locutions, and subtle bodies.

Cataloging-in-Publication Data for this title is available from the Library of Congress

ISBN 979-8-88850-144-3 (print)
ISBN 979-8-88850-145-0 (ebook)

Printed and bound in the United States by Lake Book Manufacturing, LLC

10 9 8 7 6 5 4 3 2 1

Text design and layout by Virginia Scott Bowman

This book was typeset in Garamond Premier Pro and Gill Sans with Zapf Intl ITC Std used as the display typeface

To send correspondence to the authors of this book, mail a first-class letter to the author c/o Inner Traditions • Bear & Company, One Park Street, Rochester, VT 05767, and we will forward the communication, or contact Andy Tomlinson directly at **regressionacademy@gmail.com** and Reena Kumarasingham at **divineiam@divineaspect.com**.

Scan the QR code and save 25% at InnerTraditions.com. Browse over 2,000 titles on spirituality, the occult, ancient mysteries, new science, holistic health, and natural medicine.

❖

For Dato' R. Kumarasingham

Dad

Forever the guiding light in our hearts

Contents

❖

❖

Reena's Near-Death Experience

When I was a child, my parents told me that I was born a blue baby. As I was growing inside my mother's womb, the umbilical cord twisted around my neck, strangling me. The doctors had to perform a premature C-section, and I was put in an incubator until my breathing stabilized; it was a week before my parents could even hold me. So when my near-death experience happened as a result of respiratory distress, it was almost like coming full circle.

On March 27, 2020, my father's birthday and the launch day of my second book, The Magdalene Lineage, I was deeply fatigued and had developed a fever. I could not get out of bed for a week. I thought that I was experiencing burnout.

One week later, I woke up early Tuesday morning at 3:00 a.m., and I could barely breathe. It felt as though two metal bands had been wrapped around the top and bottom of my lungs. It hurt to inhale. It was then that I realized that I had contracted COVID. I thought I was going to die and felt extremely fearful. I woke up my husband and told him I needed to either go to the hospital or have some energy work done to help me breathe. We both intuitively felt that going to the hospital would be detrimental to me, and so we opted for the energy work. I also found all the breathing exercises that I could and practiced those religiously.

The next day I found that it was easier to breathe. However, on Thursday I had a long shower and when the bathroom filled with condensation, I thought I was suffocating again. I experienced the metal band sensation around my lungs again for a short while, but it disappeared that night.

On Friday, April 10, my husband took our little Maltese terriers, bid me goodnight, and went up to his room (we slept in separate rooms during my illness). It was 10:00 p.m. when I turned off my lights. As I lay down, I felt beyond a shadow of a doubt that if I closed my eyes, I would never open them again. This awareness that I was dying came with absolute peace and calm but surprise as well.

Upon reflection now, it was interesting how thinking I was going to die had made me fearful, but knowing I was going to die filled me with the ultimate sense of peace. There was a part of my mind, however, that became hyperalert, thinking of my husband and how he would feel if he saw my lifeless body on the bed the next morning. I also wanted a minute to write a note to him saying it was not his fault, it was my time and that I loved him. I also wanted to write a to-do list for him so he'd know who to call. So, I was highly lucid and in a heightened state of awareness.

I was still in my body on my bed when I saw five beings, composed of white light and framed by a blue aura, appear at the foot of my bed. They carried out a full life review, focusing on my emotional wounding in childhood. They then worked on my heart chakra, cleared the wounding, and helped me let go of any deeply held beliefs from those wounds. As I was still in my body, this process felt very visceral, and there was a slight burning sensation in the middle of my chest. This clearing of my heart chakra left me unbound and freed from the burdens and obligations of being human. I felt that it was safe to be myself.

Then I became aware of leaving my body and bed and traveling to a place in between with the five light beings. It was a dark space filled with dots of light like the pictures you see of space. When I was moving, I felt like I was being pulled by a sudden ocean current. It was very unexpected, and I was powerless against it. There was also a very tangible feeling of separating from my ego and leaving it behind. Again, I had no choice in this matter. It happened very quickly and I was surprised by it.

I also let go of everything earthly: worries, work, everything that fed my ego—none of it was needed. What used to matter immensely to me suddenly did not matter anymore, especially the achievements and fears. But there was one thing that I did hang on to: the realization that I had not left that note for my husband.

Then we stopped and hovered in a place in between. Continuing toward the left would have taken me to an infinite space of freedom and peace. On the right was the Earth that I had just left. It was blue and had a grid of what looked like plumes of smoke from a great fire. I understood the grid to be the mass consciousness of people. Thoughts, beliefs, wounds, emotions, ideology—all suffocating the people. We create the very things that suffocate us. From this vantage point, I felt lightness within me, and I was wondering why we would create such a grid—why would we complicate such a light world? It did not make sense from that perspective. Now that I am back in this world and suffocating in the grid, it still does not make sense, but I am not as detached from it as I was before.

I was then given a quick lesson that time is infinite and that Earth will keep turning long after humans have left. Earth will shake off this grid and be free. It is not humanity that determines the health or shift or path of Earth. Earth is a ground for humankind to experience the *gifts of emotion and the challenges of evolution. It's not that Earth needs humankind; humankind needs Earth—humanity chooses Earth.*

At this point, I was given a choice—to leave or to live. To leave was to go to that place of amazing freedom and peace on the left. To live was to return to Earth. My memory of how long it took for me to ponder this question is hazy. I remember feeling how incredibly tempting it would be to leave—to go to the left, to a place of infinite peace and freedom.

But I chose to live. I chose to live in that state of freedom and peace in the pockets on Earth not suffocated by the black plume of smoke, the grid of consciousness. I chose the challenge of bringing the freedom and expansiveness of that space to Earth.

I became lucid and alert again, and I remember thinking, I want to live, I choose to live. Then the light beings pulled white aspects out of my body. I am not sure what they were. I am guessing they were the worst of the symptoms perhaps.

Then everything went dark. When I woke up and looked at the time, it was 2:00 a.m. I spent the rest of the night in a state of mild shock. In my conscious mind, all I knew was that I almost died. The next morning, my husband came in to say hi, and I told him, shocking him too.

It took a while for me to get better after that. Not only was my body healing from COVID, but my being was changing and healing from this intense experience, and my heart chakra was healing from the clearing work. It took a long time for me to process what had happened. It wasn't until two months after the incident that I accepted that I'd had a near-death experience. My brush with death was certainly life changing and is not one that I will ever forget.

As I was slowly processing my near-death experience, I realized just how similar the process was to between lives spiritual regression (also known as Life Between Lives regression). Having been a between lives spiritual regression trainer for the Past Life Regression Academy for almost ten years, training in the UK, the United States, Australia, and Asia, the similarities between my near-death experience journey and the between lives spiritual regression process that I teach surprised me.

The preceding description was Reena's account of her near-death experience, which had such a big impact on us both that we decided to investigate it. Was it just a fluke experience? Was it related to the eternal soul and reincarnation? What scientific research has been done in this area?

For many years, we had both worked with clients therapeutically, and when they were regressed with the right prompting, stories emerged that appeared to be past lives and the soul's memories of what occurred between lives. We are both psychologists and have an interest in the eternal soul and the scientific research that supports consciousness existing outside the brain—an idea that directly challenges the materialist views of consciousness and the soul. So together we have written this book, which looks deeply into consciousness and the evolution of the eternal soul.

In part one we explore consciousness and the evidence that strongly suggests it is an independent state that survives the body after death. Having established what consciousness is and what the experiences of being between lives and near death are like, we move on to part two, which is a guide to expanding consciousness and developing the wisdom needed for an awakening world. We also explore what this all means to us as we begin living in the New Consciousness and ultimately create a New Earth.

PART ONE

What Is Consciousness and Does It Survive Physical Death?

1
Consciousness

I regard consciousness as fundamental. I regard matter as a derivative from consciousness. . . . Everything that we talk about, everything that we regard as existing, postulates consciousness. . . . There is no matter as such. All matter originates and exists only by virtue of a force which brings the particle of an atom to vibration and holds this most minute solar system of the atom together. We must assume behind this force is the existence of a conscious and intelligent mind.

MAX PLANCK

———————— ◆ ————————

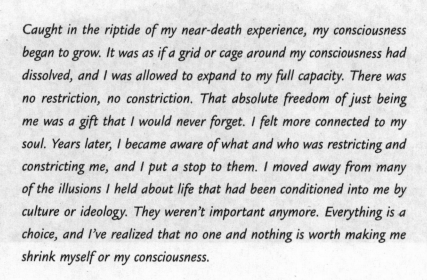

Caught in the riptide of my near-death experience, my consciousness began to grow. It was as if a grid or cage around my consciousness had dissolved, and I was allowed to expand to my full capacity. There was no restriction, no constriction. That absolute freedom of just being me was a gift that I would never forget. I felt more connected to my soul. Years later, I became aware of what and who was restricting and constricting me, and I put a stop to them. I moved away from many of the illusions I held about life that had been conditioned into me by culture or ideology. They weren't important anymore. Everything is a choice, and I've realized that no one and nothing is worth making me shrink myself or my consciousness.

This was a summary of Reena's near-death experience and opens the question of what is consciousness? On the journey to examine consciousness, we touch upon the neuroscientific and parapsychology fields of study. We then dive deep into the areas of near-death experience, past life regression, and between lives regression to investigate the similarities that Reena noticed in her own experiences. As part of this study, we have conducted new research that compares hundreds of accounts of near-death experience and between lives regression to investigate the similarities of conscious experience after death. Does consciousness survive death or was Reena's experience a one-off happening?

While some will see it as an interesting academic or philosophical debate, we noticed that Reena's life changed drastically after her near-death experience, which had jump-started an evolution of her consciousness and ignited a new way of being. It's led her to live with intention. Many others who have gone through such a profound episode have also experienced a powerful transformation. So it got us thinking . . . Is something as extreme as death or a near-death experience needed to evolve consciousness? We think that the answer is a resounding no! While death in all its forms fast-tracks our evolution, we can evolve and lead an intentional life right now, if we truly commit to it. The second part of this book provides guidance and exercises for expanding our consciousness to help us do just that.

THE CONSCIOUSNESS DEBATE

Within the materialist paradigm, scientists have been grappling with how the brain produces consciousness. Francis Crick, one of the codiscoverers of the molecular structure of DNA, proposed that a person's mental activities are entirely due to the behavior of nerve cells, and that the atoms and molecules that make up the nerve cells produce consciousness. In a similar way, Marvin Minsky, an American computer scientist known for his work with artificial intelligence, likened humans to machines. But neither of these materialist views of consciousness can explain Reena's near-death experience, which seems to directly challenge their validity. It seems consciousness is bigger and wider than just our neurophysiology, and perhaps our brain is merely the vessel that receives and transmits consciousness. As yet there is no definitive scientific proof in the fields of quantum physics or neuroscience of the survival of human consciousness after permanent bodily death. However, within the field of parapsychology, there has been an increasing amount of study in the areas of telepathy, mediumship, out-of-body experiences, and terminal lucidity that is providing compelling evidence that consciousness does exist outside our physical anatomical structures.

SAVANT SYNDROME AND GENIUS

To understand the mystifying nature of consciousness the first two areas we will look at are genius and savant syndrome. Genius describes someone who has exceptional intellectual or creative power. Often this is because the person has an unusual brain. For instance, at three years old, Wolfgang Amadeus Mozart was picking out chords on the harpsichord, and at four he was playing short pieces of music. There are also anecdotes about his precise memory of pitch and scribbling down music to a concert at the age of five.[1] What could explain this impressive ability at such a young age? Is it possible that he brought the ability with him from a past life or perhaps that he tuned in to a spiritual source of information in some way?

Savant syndrome takes it further. This is a rare condition of people with a developmental disorder who have an astonishing area of ability or brilliance that stands in marked contrast to their overall limitations. Kim Peek, for example, the inspiration for the character of Raymond Babbitt in the 1988 movie *Rain Man*, can read a book from cover to cover in around an hour, completely memorizing the content for rapid and accurate recall. So far, he has memorized over ten thousand books.[2]

Another example is Stephen Wiltshire, an artist with autism who can draw cityscapes in stunning detail. On one occasion in 2001 he appeared in a BBC documentary called *Fragments of Genius* in which he was filmed flying over London aboard a helicopter. Over the next five days, using only his memory, he drew the seven-square-mile panorama on a thirteen-foot curving canvas. He did not refer to notes, preliminary sketches, or photographs, and his drawing included the precise number of skyscraper floors.[3]

Perhaps people with savant syndrome, like those who are considered geniuses, can be explained away as having a special brain. But could there be other factors of consciousness involved? As we continue in this chapter it will be useful to keep an open mind so you can begin to understand what consciousness really is.

LUCID DREAMING

Dreams take us to a different reality, a hallucinatory world that feels as real as any waking experience. These episodes that occur during human sleep have yet to be adequately explained. One of the most interesting types is called lucid dreaming, which is when a person is aware that they are dreaming, and they have some level of control over what happens in the dream.

A pioneer in this area is Karen Konkoly, who has a doctorate in brain behavior and cognition. She has led teams of independent researchers in the United States, Netherlands, Germany, and France and was able to demonstrate that two-way communication with lucid dreamers is possible.

The researchers implemented the procedures for two-way communication during verified sleep in thirty-six subjects. Some had minimal prior experience with lucid dreaming, while others were frequent lucid dreamers. In these studies, the lucid dreamers were able to follow instructions to compute mathematical operations, answer yes-or-no questions, and discriminate stimuli in the visual, tactile, and auditory modalities while asleep. They responded using distinctive eye movements and selective facial muscle contractions. They also correctly answered questions on twenty-nine occasions, and this was confirmed by all four independent laboratory groups.[4]

One of the criticisms of this study is that it is possible that some subjects may have flickered to being partially awake to answer the questions. However, a 2009 study by Ursula Voss[5] showed that lucid dreaming constitutes a state of consciousness that has measurable differences from both our waking consciousness and the rapid eye movement sleep. This study showed that lucid dreamers operate within gamma brain waves, which are of the highest frequency range (from 30–40 Hz) and quite a bit above the wide-awake alpha state of the brain (from 3–13 Hz), which is a totally different level of consciousness.

This suggests that to understand consciousness we need to include other realities such as lucid dreams.

TELEPATHIC COMMUNICATION

We now move from studies of lucid dreaming to evidence that suggests consciousness exists outside of the body. Investigation of the special state of consciousness during sleep was taken further to see if telepathy was also possible with sleeping subjects. After several years of pilot studies Montague Ullman, a psychiatrist and parapsychologist, launched the Dream Laboratory at the Maimonides Medical Center in New York in 1962. This purpose-built laboratory enabled subjects' brain activity to be monitored while asleep.[6]

Typically, a sender in a nearby room would attempt to telepathically transmit an image to the person sleeping in the dream laboratory. When instruments indicated that the sleeper was in a rapid eye movement period and assumed to be dreaming, the subject would be woken and asked to describe their dream imagery. The following day the dreamer would view a pool of art prints that included the target image and rank them according to how closely they resembled the previous night's dream. The selections reviewed by independent judges were scored in a binary manner as either a hit (ranked in the top 50 percent) or a miss (ranked in the bottom 50 percent).

An analysis of more than 450 trials conducted throughout the Maimonides research program showed the overall combined hit rate was 63 percent, where only 50 percent would be expected by chance.[7] These results are highly significant, with the probability of them being coincidental about 75 million to one. The advantage of the Maimonides studies was that they could awaken subjects during rapid eye movement sleep, immediately after the telepathy test, which led to them having more information and detailed reports.

MEDIUMSHIP

I started my career in the computer industry, so all my beliefs were based on an analytical and rational explanation of life that did not include a spiritual aspect. In my early forties, I visited my sister in Lowestoft in the UK, and she suggested that I see a medium who was highly regarded. I was skeptical but at the same time curious. When I went for my reading, I met with an elderly rather large white-haired man whom I had never seen before. One of the first things he said was, "Spirits are telling me you were never happy playing rugby at school, were you?" At school, for some reason, I was always picked to be in the rugby first team during the winter when it was cold and muddy and the fields were frozen, and I always hoped I would not be picked. Yet I never told my sister, any family members, or anyone else and hadn't thought about the subject for over twenty years. So, where did this information come from?

The medium then went on to say, "There is a lady in a spiritualist church close to where you live waiting to work with you." In the UK, a spiritualist church is where people meet once a week and focus on proving the survival of consciousness after death through mediums channeling information to those in attendance. My first thought was, I'm in charge of what I do, and I dismissed the information.

A few months later while at home the memory of this popped into my mind, so I decided to test it. It turned out that there were three spiritualist churches in the area, so I picked one and found out when the next service was. I walked into the church not knowing what to expect and within a few minutes an elderly lady came up to me who I had never seen before and said, "You must be Andy. My spirit guide said you would be coming but was not sure how long it would take."

It turned out that the elderly lady was a clairvoyant—a little like a medium but instead of channeling information from deceased loved ones, she channeled information from evolved spirits of light. On one occasion she said that their message to me was that I would be working with people lying down and that the Cathars would be significant for me. At the time I did not understand this message but several years later, when I left the computer industry and became a psychotherapist specializing in regression therapy, I realized that my clients lie down for therapy, and my work included regressing them to past lives—something that the Cathars believed in.

The account above describes Andy's early experience of receiving channeled information from spirits that changed his life and set him on a spiritual path.

Communication with the deceased is an aspect of cultures all over the world and something that could perhaps provide proof of the survival of consciousness after permanent bodily death. Although it is possible for anyone to experience communication from a deceased person, a medium is someone who does this regularly and reliably on demand.

The practice of doing this work can be traced to primeval times, where shamans in early communities provided guidance to their tribe through communication with the spirit world. Today, while there are some very accurate mediums, there are many that are either less accurate or fakes.

The first attempts to carry out scientific research started in 1882 with the founding members of the Society for Psychical Research. Their studies tailed off in the 1930s but interest in the subject began again in the 2000s. Although there have been several recent researchers, one of the most prominent is Gary Schwartz, an American psychologist and professor at the University of Arizona and the director of its Laboratory for Advances in Consciousness and Health. He had several research projects where he claimed he was able to demonstrate the accuracy of mediums obtaining information about recently deceased relatives.[8]

The criticism of Schwartz's work is very similar to that other researchers in this area have experienced—namely, that mediums often throw out streams of general information and follow up on those that they get a visible reaction from. Another is the subjective validation of ambiguous or multiple-choice statements. For example, "I am getting a name that starts with an *M* or an *R*." This may fit any of several deceased friends or relatives.[9]

Another difficulty is that communication could be coming via telepathy from the mind of the subject. Or the communication could be coming from the collective unconscious that Carl Jung proposed was a universal database that people can tap into telepathically.

However, interesting research was conducted by Arnaud Delorme at the Institute of Noetic Sciences in California in 2013.[10] Delorme, together with his team, performed controlled tests with six mediums that had previously given accurate readings under double-blind conditions. The mediums were asked to think about a living person they knew, then think about a fabricated person, listen to information spoken by an experimenter, and then mentally interact with a deceased person. This was done while their brain activity was monitored with an electroencephalogram (EEG). These are small sensors that attach to the scalp to pick up the electrical signals produced by brain cells. The study's findings suggested that a mental state occurred during communication with the deceased person that was unlike any of the states that occurred during the other scenarios and was different from normal thinking or imagination.

This was small-scale research and would need to be expanded to get more meaningful results and possibly extended to using magnetic resonance imaging (MRI). This is a type of scan that uses strong magnetic fields and radio waves that would produce very detailed images of the activated parts of a medium's brain.

Medium communication with the deceased is a fascinating area of study that could very well establish the existence of the survival of consciousness after death, but protocols with mediums need to be more tightly managed to obtain more substantial and credible findings. For the time being we need to rely on anecdotal accounts or our own experience with a medium.

OUT-OF-BODY EXPERIENCES

An out-of-body experience, also called an OBE, is the sense of having separated from one's physical body and sometimes viewing it from the outside. This can happen spontaneously during a life-threatening situation and will be discussed in the next chapter. However, some people report that by conscious intent or through drugs or in deep hypnosis or while dreaming, they can have an out-of-body experience. When this involves experiences thought to be in spiritual dimensions or the afterlife it is called astral traveling.

An influential researcher in this area was Robert Monroe, who wrote the bestselling book *Journeys Out of the Body*[11] and later founded the Monroe Institute. He was keen to prove that his out-of-body traveling was not just imagination. So, he developed an experiment where he set the intention to visit an ill friend who lived nearby in a bedroom he had never seen before. He hoped to obtain accurate descriptions of what he viewed remotely in the house that could later be verified. Some of the details he obtained, including the clothes of the doctor's wife, were later confirmed.

Although a number of remote viewing research studies have been done by individual researchers, a majority of them have been done in three laboratories: the Stanford Research Institute in Palo Alto, California, the Princeton Engineering Anomalies Research Lab at Princeton University in New Jersey, and the Mobius Society Laboratory in Los Angeles, California.

An independent review of the research by the American Institutes for Research found that statistically significant results of remote viewing occurred more often than by chance.[12] However, it was unclear that the observed effects could unambiguously be attributed to the ability of the remote viewers as opposed to characteristics of the judges.

Susan Blackmore, a professor at the University of Plymouth in the UK, carried out a postal questionnaire of 593 randomly selected people and, of the 321 who responded, 12 percent reported they had had an out-of-body experience. Most occurred when resting but not asleep and lasted one to five minutes. The state of consciousness that these people were in during the out-of-body experience was split between it being like they were awake or like they were dreaming. Less than half claimed to have traveled away from their body, and those who could see their own physical body found it looked normal. While there was no information about remote viewing in this research, it does suggest that out-of-body experiences are more common than might be expected.[13]

One of the first comprehensive written reports of experiencing the afterlife through astral travel was by Emanuel Swedenborg in the eighteenth century.[14] As a child he would relax, close his eyes, and focus with total concentration on a scientific problem. He created a deep meditation rather like a hypnosis trance. In this state his breathing would nearly stop and his awareness of the outer world and even bodily sensation would diminish to the point of vanishing. His whole existence would focus on the one issue he wanted to understand. He did this twice a day and what began as an intellectual form of meditation progressed to an exploration of his dreams. He then learned to explore what he believed was the afterlife and wrote several books on his experiences.

Several other authors have written books about their astral traveling experiences in the afterlife, which they did by conscious intent like Swedenborg, but for most people these attempts are not successful.[15]

Although astral travel may be another fascinating area that could provide proof that consciousness resides outside the body, it unfortunately lacks objective verification or peer-reviewed research, unlike near-death experiences, which will be discussed in later chapters.

A SHARED DEATH EXPERIENCE

A shared death experience is an interesting aspect of consciousness and has been reported by healthy people who are present at the bedside of a dying relative and who apparently share some aspect of the death experience with the person who is dying. They occasionally see an incredibly special light in the room or around the bed of the dying person and experience qualities of bliss, compassion, and unconditional love. And sometimes they join the death experience of the person who just died and then are suddenly back in their body again at their bedside. The following account was from a case study from Pim van Lommel's book *Consciousness Beyond Life*:[16]

I was in a relationship with Anne when she suddenly died in a serious traffic accident. Her son, who'd just turned seven, sustained severe head trauma. His brain virtually spilled out of his skull—it looked like a smashed watermelon—and it took him about five days to make the transition [to die]. He was the eldest grandson of a couple with nine children. Some sixty relatives had gathered around his hospital bed, and since I'd only been his mother's boyfriend, I was standing somewhere at the back by the window.

The moment he died, when his EEG flatlined, I "saw" that his mother came to collect him. You must bear in mind that she'd died five days earlier. There was this incredibly beautiful reunion. And at one point they reached out for me and included me in their embrace. This was an indescribable, ecstatic reunion. Part of me left my body and accompanied them to the light. I know this must sound very strange indeed, but I was fully conscious and with Anne and her son as they went to the light, just as I was fully conscious and in the room where all the relatives were incredibly sad because their nephew and grandson had just died. And I joined them, we were heading toward

the light, but at a certain point it was clear that I had to return, so I
fell back. I simply fell back into my body.

It was such an overwhelming experience, I glowed with
happiness, but then I suddenly realized that I had a big smile on
my face amid all these people who'd just lost a child dear to them.
I quickly covered my face with my hands because I didn't want to
be disrespectful toward all these mourning and crying people in the
room. And I never said a word about the experience. Talking about
it seemed completely inappropriate at the time, and besides, I didn't
have the words to describe what had happened to me. I used to
think that I knew what was what. But my worldview underwent a
radical transformation.

This seems to be an example of spontaneous telepathic communication. As there does not appear to be any research to establish the frequency of shared death experiences, for the time being we need to rely on anecdotal accounts.

TERMINAL LUCIDITY

Terminal lucidity happens when people who are in a coma or are experiencing Alzheimer's, dementia, or other conditions where the brain is not working normally become completely lucid for hours or days just before they die. They have a full memory and know who they are talking to and can reminisce on past experiences. It has been reported in the medical literature over the past 250 years but has received little attention. A team led by Michael Nahm, a German biologist and parapsychologist, reviewed a range of terminal lucidity cases including patients suffering from brain abscesses, tumors, strokes, meningitis, dementia, or Alzheimer's disease, schizophrenia, and affective disorders.[17]

An example of terminal lucidity comes from an article published in *Time* magazine by Dr. Scott Haig, an assistant clinical professor of orthopedic surgery.[18] When Dr. Haig saw David, a brain scan revealed that David's head was full of cancer, and he hardly had any brain left. He had stopped speaking and moving, and eventually he stopped responding to anything the medical team did.

Haig reported, "It was particularly bad in the room that Friday when I made evening rounds. The family was there, sad, crying faces on all of them. . . . His respirations had become agonal—the gulping kind of breathing movement that immediately precedes death." The next time Haig checked, the bed was empty and made up with clean fresh sheets. An Irish nurse who had taken care of David that night said, "He woke up, you know, doctor—just after you left—and said goodbye to them all. Like I'm talkin' to you right here. Like a miracle. He talked to them and patted them and smiled for about five minutes. Then he went out again, and he passed in the hour."

What had woken David and how could he have had a rational conversation with no brain? Could it be that his eternal soul or consciousness had bypassed the brain to communicate one last time with his family?

There has been little formal research done to understand how common this type of experience is. According to Nahm, cases of terminal lucidity have been recorded for millennia, from accounts by classical scholars such as Hippocrates, Cicero, and Plutarch to nineteenth-century medical luminaries like Benjamin Rush. By the twentieth century, he speculates, doctors simply stopped reporting these incidents altogether because they failed to fit in with scientific materialism. However, in one study, 70 percent of support staff in a British nursing home who responded to a questionnaire said they'd personally observed people with dementia becoming lucid shortly before their deaths.[19]

These accounts suggest that during terminal lucidity, memory and cognitive abilities may function through consciousness outside the brain. This is another piece of the puzzle of human consciousness.

SUMMARY OF CHAPTER I

Perhaps consciousness can be described as what we experience with our senses, the positive and negative emotions of life and the experience of images, ideas, words, and thoughts. Evan Harris Walker, in his book *The Physics of Consciousness*, likened consciousness to an image on a television: The set is the body, the electronics are the brain, and the image on the set is our consciousness.[20] The image is not part of the television or the light from the screen. It is all around it and what we experience. Likewise, consciousness is all around us regardless of whether we have a brain to receive and transmit it.

If consciousness exists even without a brain to receive, perceive, and transmit it, then it is only reasonable to postulate that consciousness continues after the death of the physical body, much like the image on a television can continue to be transmitted on other television sets once the current set has expired. So perhaps our consciousness is an aspect of the eternal soul?

2
Near-Death Experiences

Death is a favor to us,
But our scales have lost their balance.
The impermanence of the body
Should give us great clarity,
Deepening the wonder in our senses and eyes
Of this mysterious existence we share
And are surely just traveling through.

HAFIZ, FOURTEENTH-CENTURY
PERSIAN MYSTIC AND POET

———————— ✧ ————————

In October of 1987 . . . I proceeded to shoot two bags of heroin mixed with some cocaine I had with me . . . I vaguely remember being carried into the house, and . . . trying to be revived with water, ice, and slapping of the face. Now is when the NDE [near-death experience] begins its journey to the light. . . .

As I looked down watching my physical body turn purple, blue, and then gray, I remember saying to myself [while out of the body], This time, Pat, you really did it. There was a part of me, like a sixth sense, that knew, This time you really are dying after countless times of coming so, so close. I knew what was happening and with such amazing awareness—watching myself from above still smaller only to see and hear all the paramedics work on me . . . I heard them say on the telephone to the hospital, "We're not getting a pulse; we're losing her." I wasn't even upset that I was dying because the next thing I remember happening was that I was floating away . . . in a dimension of total peace and serenity. . . . The light was the brightest and most brilliant I had ever seen both before my NDE and since. The light was more brilliant than a diamond.

I kept going toward the light and when I was about two-thirds of the way there I had a multidimensional sense, a feeling of seeing my left-behind body, having my past life flash in front of me, and at this point seeing stairs. . . . I only got so far and then the trip to the light ended at the bottom part of this plateau castle. The scenes of my life kept flashing before me, scene after scene, event after event zipped by right in front of me. It was like watching a movie without the projector and screen.

This all happened so fast, yet being dead for almost three minutes doesn't seem time enough for all the events to have happened. . . . Then, just as I felt I found the feeling of total love, acceptance, and peace and serenity, I was being told that I had to come back, there were things I still had to do.

All of a sudden, I jolted back into the physical left-behind body, flopping like a fish. . . . My initial reaction was, What's this? I realized I was back on this Earth, alive. I figured I should be overwhelmed, yet I wasn't. . . . I didn't have any verbal words when I went to the light, but I do know that I was forgiven for all the wrongs I had done and the thoughts and feelings turned into words before I was to return. I was returning to hear and, more important, to feel that I . . . still have things to do.

I finally got myself together. I am a recovering addict that unless you knew me before, you would never know that I had such a life of

despair. I am now a happy, good-hearted, honest, wholesome person. I
have this inner peace about me that is incredible. I attribute the way I
am now to my NDE. . . . I am pretty psychic. I seem to know so much
more than before. Nothing that happens seems to amaze me. . . . I
am so aware of things, people, and animals. Anything that is a part of
this universe I feel so connected to, from trees to stars. I have a special
interest in astronomy. I find great pleasure with natural things in my
life. I go with my vibes that never get me in any type of trouble [but]
instead make me more confident and reassure me of what's right.

The preceding account is an extract from a letter written by Pat Clark to Kenneth Ring, a professor of psychology at the University of Connecticut who was researching near-death experiences. The letter was published in the *Journal of Near-Death Studies*.[1] Pat was thirty-five years old at the time of her near-death experience and had been abusing drugs for twenty-three years.

A near-death experience can describe any life-threatening event but is normally applied to a cluster of experiences reported by people who have survived a potentially fatal accident or illness. In Pat's case study she appeared to be physically dead from the overdose yet was able to look at down at her body. How could this be if consciousness is within the brain and only exists when the physical body is alive? Furthermore, the three-minute experience was so dramatic it totally changed her life, gave her new abilities, such as being more psychic, and left her a happy wholesome person.

To establish how common a near-death experience is, George Gallup undertook a survey of 1,500 adult Americans using his normal polling methods between early 1980 and September 1981 and published them in his book *Adventures in Immortality*.[2] He made a projection that of 160 million adult Americans, 8 million could have had a near-death experience.

Kenneth Ring set out to provide a substantial scientific foundational basis for the near-death experience. He introduced sampling procedures, comparison groups, and quantifying variables.[3] Together with his staff, he interviewed more than a hundred people who had come close to death. All but two were clearly unconscious or comatose at the time of their near-death experience. The aspects they investigated included the incidence of near-death experiences, whether near-death experiences are influenced by the circumstances that cause them, and the possible influence of religious beliefs. They also compared near-death experiences reported during suicide attempts, illnesses, and accidents and went on to investigate the phenomenon of subsequent life changes. He found that just under 50 percent of his sample had experienced some aspect of near-death experience.

Ring also proposed an ordered sequence of ten stages as an additional indicator of the depth of a near-death experience. These included the sense of being dead, feelings of peace and well-being, an awareness of being separated from the body, entering a darkness, encountering a presence, hearing a voice, taking stock of their life, being enveloped by and entering the light, seeing beautiful colors, and encountering visible spirits.

NEAR-DEATH EXPERIENCES
OF BLIND PEOPLE

Another early medical researcher in the field of near-death experience studies included cardiologist Michael Sabom. In 1976, Sabom and his social-worker colleague, Sarah Kreutziger, began asking patients who had survived a medical crisis if they recalled anything that happened during that experience. In this study, it was estimated that 27 percent of the seventy-eight patients who survived a near-death medical crisis had had a near-death experience. One of these cases, which is noted in

Sabom's book *Recollections of Death*,[4] was a soldier who was blind at the time. He was an American veteran of the Vietnam War who had been almost fatally wounded in a mine explosion. He had lost both legs and an arm and lost his sight for three weeks. His near-death experience began to unfold while he lay unconscious just after the explosion and continued when he went into surgery.

He remembered the battlefield scene when he came out of his body and saw himself lying on the ground with three limbs gone. After surgery, he talked about the events: "I was able to look at my body and see a tube pushed down my mouth. And then I saw them cut my uniform off and start whatever fluid they have to start. At the time my left leg was cut off. It was only hanging on by a piece of skin."

Someone who is blind at the time of a near-death experience and can still "see" events as they happen to their bodies is a fascinating area and the subject of research by Kenneth Ring. Ring's investigation included fourteen people who were blind from birth, and nine of them described highly visual content consistent with typical near-death experiences. The following are some examples from his book *Mindsight: Near-Death and Out-of-Body Experiences in the Blind*:[5]

"The first thing I was aware of is that I was up on the ceiling and I heard this doctor talking and looked down and I saw this body and at first, I was not sure that it was my own. But I recognized my hair."

"Things were extremely clear. I mean I could literally see everything around me for such a distance that I could not believe."

"I had no sight because I had total destruction of my eyes in the accident, but it was very clear and distinct. . . . I had perfect vision in that experience."

The fact that blind people are able to see during a near-death experience, particularly when the details are subjected to objective verification, further suggests that consciousness is outside the body and not a hallucinatory experience.

NEAR-DEATH EXPERIENCE
WITH NO BRAIN ACTIVITY

In some cases the person experiencing the near-death experience has been monitored by medical staff who report a flat EEG, indicating an absence of electrical activity in the cerebral cortex, resulting in a significant reduction of brain functioning. In this state, sensory organs are nonfunctional and so is the brain's capacity to process their signals.

An example is the near-death experience of Pam Reynolds, reported in Michael Sabom's book *Light and Death: One Doctor's Fascinating Account of Near-Death Experiences*.[6] Pam was an American singer-songwriter whose near-death experience happened when her brain and body functions were completely shut down to allow for surgery on a brain aneurysm. Blood was removed, chilled, and returned to her body. As her core temperature fell, her heart stopped and her brain waves ceased, which met the definition of clinical death. In the low temperature, her body was able to survive for two hours while the surgery was completed. Later, while recovering, she recalled accurate views of the operating room and interactions with deceased relatives. During the operation, the song "Hotel California" had been playing, and she mentioned remembering a line of the music being played.

Criticism of this account suggested that Reynolds retained sufficient conscious awareness even under anesthesia to hear the "Hotel California" song. But according to Sabom, the technologist who inserted the ear plugs into Pam's ears used tape and gauze to keep them in place that covered the entire ear entrance, which made normal hearing of any music or conversation in the operating room impossible. In addition, with her heart stopped and all brain wave activities ceased, how had she recalled the events of the experience unless her consciousness was outside the body?

NEAR-DEATH EXPERIENCE
DURING CARDIAC ARREST

Pim van Lommel studied medicine at Utrecht University and then specialized in cardiology for twenty-six years at the Rijnstate Hospital in Arnhem, a city in the Netherlands. Together with colleagues he carried out a comprehensive near-death experience study over thirteen years, during which time they investigated the experiences of 344 patients in ten Dutch hospitals who had been resuscitated after a cardiac arrest. They compared the demographic, medical, pharmacological, and psychological data of the patients who reported a near-death experience. They also had patients who did not report near-death experiences as a control group. In 2001, his large-scale prospective study into near-death experiences after cardiac arrest was published in the Lancet medical journal.[7] The following is an example reported by van Lommel:

During a night shift an ambulance brought in a 44-year-old cyanotic, comatose man into the coronary care unit. He had been found about an hour before in a meadow by passers-by. After admission, he received artificial respiration, heart massage and defibrillation. He had dentures in his mouth that were removed and put into a "crash car." Then extensive cardiopulmonary resuscitation (CPR) was performed. After about an hour and a half the patient had sufficient heart rhythm and blood pressure but was still comatose. He was transferred to the intensive care unit to continue the necessary artificial respiration.

After more than a week the patient was back on the cardiac ward. The nurse involved with the resuscitation was distributing his medication when he said, "You know where my dentures are. Yes, you were there when I was brought into hospital and you took my dentures out of my mouth and put them onto that car, it had all these bottles on it and

there was this sliding drawer underneath and there you put my teeth."
The nurse was amazed because she remembered this happening while
the man was in a deep coma and in the process of CPR.

   It appeared the man had seen himself lying in bed, that he had
perceived from above how nurses and doctors had been busy with CPR.
He was also able to describe correctly and in detail the small room
in which he had been resuscitated as well as the appearance of those
present like myself. At the time that he observed the situation he had
been very much afraid that we would stop CPR and that he would die.
He was deeply impressed by his experience and said he was no longer
afraid of death. Four weeks later he left hospital as a healthy man.

COMMUNICATION DURING
A NEAR-DEATH EXPERIENCE

Jack was a twenty-five-year-old technical writer in South Africa, and his
case was recalled by Bruce Greyson, a former professor of psychiatry at the
University of Virginia in a talk to the Scientific and Medical Network.[8]

Jack was hospitalized with severe pneumonia and had repeated
respiratory arrest episodes where he couldn't breathe and had to be
resuscitated repeatedly. He was hospitalized for several weeks with
this. And he had one primary nurse who worked with him every day;
she was about his age, and they got to know each other very well. One
day she told him she was going to be taking a long weekend off. He
said farewell to her and wished her well over the weekend.

   Later he had another respiratory arrest where he had to be
resuscitated. During that event he had a near-death experience. He
found himself in a beautiful pastoral scene, with a beautiful meadow
with flowers and trees and the forest in the background. Then to his
surprise he saw his primary nurse come walking to him out of the

forest across the middle, and he was startled when she said, "What
are you doing here? This is where I live now, but you can't stay here.
You need to go back to your body. I want you to find my parents. I
want you to tell them I love them very much. And I'm sorry that I
wrecked the red MGB." The image turned and walked away.

When Jack recovered, he had a complete vivid memory of this
experience, and he excitedly tried to tell the other nurses that came
into his room, but they didn't want to hear it. It turned out that his
primary nurse, taking the weekend off to celebrate her twenty-first
birthday, had been surprised with a gift of a red MGB. She got very
excited, jumped into the car, took off for a drive, lost control of it, and
crashed into a telephone pole and died. This happened a few hours
before Jack's near-death experience. There was no way that he could
have known that she had died or how it happened.

The only explanation in this case seems that some part of the nurse
survived her death and was able to communicate meaningfully to Jack
after she died. Jack's near-death experience occurred four or five hours
after she died, so this suggests that consciousness survives at least this
length of time.

Greyson was raised in a scientific household, and his father was
a chemist. While he was growing up, the physical world was all there
was for him. However, as a psychiatrist in the 1980s, he ran support
groups for patients, many of whom talked about out-of-body experiences, which he tried to make sense of. He was faced with a growing
number of stories of people experiencing otherworldly events, either
when they had been pronounced clinically dead or had thought they
were close to it before being wrestled back to life.

Inspired by Jack's account and many other similar ones, Greyson
went on to do research on near-death experiences with seventy-four
subjects, publish more than one hundred near-death experience articles

in academic, medical, and psychological journals, and edit three books. He was also given several research grants and awards.

THE IMPACT OF A
NEAR-DEATH EXPERIENCE

Suddenly, not knowing how or why, I returned to my broken body. But miraculously, I brought back the love and the joy. I was filled with an ecstasy beyond my wildest dreams. Here, in my body, the pain had all been removed. I was still enthralled by a boundless delight. For the next two months I remained in this state, oblivious to any pain. I wonder now if this were not the purpose behind the experience—to enable me to get through this period of recovery.

I felt now as if I had been made anew. I saw wondrous meanings everywhere; everything was alive and full of energy and intelligence. My sister, who visited me shortly after the accident, tells me that I once took her down to the ocean's edge, pointed up to the sky, and tried to show her the path that was inscribed there. She thought that I was either mad or on drugs!

I don't remember too much of this period, except that I did some things that were, for me, incredible. In the past I had been painfully shy and had felt myself unworthy of being loved. I went out, my head swathed in bandages like a creature from a horror film, landed a job in one week, made many friends, and got involved in my first serious romantic relationship. After the earthquake in 1971, I moved back East, went home to my mother, with whom I became reconciled, and started college at 23, another thing I never thought I could handle. Since then, I have married, become a mother, pursued a career, and have sipped deeply from the cup of life's blessings that I had never believed would come my way in those dark years before I found the Light.

The preceding was the account of Beverly Brodsky, who in 1970 suffered a fractured skull and had a near-death experience reported by Kenneth Ring in the *Journal of Near-Death Studies.* Her experience included reentering the body and the impact it had on her.[9]

For many, the near-death experience is intense and life-changing in a positive way. From their experiences it seems that loving others is of momentous significance and importance for life on Earth. Pim van Lommel did follow-up interviews two and eight years later with his 344 near-death experience subjects.[10] He revealed that the subjects' behaviors and attitudes changed as a direct result of their near-death experience and that these changes increased with time. He identified the following changes:

+ Reduced fear of death
+ Increased compassion
+ Heightened sense of intuitive feeling
+ Greater involvement in family life
+ Greater interest in spirituality
+ Reduced interest in acquiring money, possessions, and conforming to social norms
+ Experiences of clairvoyance, premonitions, and visions
+ Acceptance of others
+ Appreciation of ordinary things

The other pioneers like Ring and Greyson found similarities in their research, particularly in the life-changing and long-lasting impact of a near-death experience. In addition, Greyson, who as a psychiatrist worked with suicidal patients, was surprised to find them less suicidal following a near-death experience.[11]

To understand how real the near-death experiences were for people, Dr. Helena Cassol and her team in the Consciousness and Neurology

Department at the University Hospital of Liège, worked with twenty-five near-death experience subjects to compare the personal impact of the experience with autobiographical current-life memories and flash-bulb memories (memories with a highly emotional content that are remembered for most of a person's life).[12] They found the near-death experience memories were more central to a person's identity than autobiographical or flashbulb memories. This highlights the uniqueness of near-death memories.

ALTERNATIVE VIEWS

Many other researchers offer alternative theories to the near-death experience. For instance, English parapsychologist Susan Blackmore proposed that as blood flow slows down and oxygen levels fall (anoxia), the brain cells fire one last electrical impulse.[13] The process starts in one part of the brain and spreads in a cascade. Blackmore suggested that this firing of neurons is responsible for visual perception and may give people vivid mental sensations that possibly lead to the experience of a white light at the end of a tunnel. However, if Blackmore's thesis is true, all survivors of cardiac arrest would be expected to report the tunnel effect, and this is not the case, as the reports of transition are varied. Also, the onset of anoxia typically results in an acutely confused state that allows patients very little recall of events. It contrasts sharply with the lucid thought processes and heightened state of awareness experienced during a near-death experience.

Neuroscientist Olaf Blanke proposed that the sensation of being outside the body can result from electrical stimulation of the angular gyrus within the brain.[14] Pim van Lommel refuted that claim by arguing that the experiences induced during Blanke's experiments led to a false sense of reality, which is different from the heightened state of awareness described by people who have a near-death experience.

Greyson noted that evidence that the brain can stimulate out-of-body-like illusions cannot be held as proof that all out-of-body experiences are illusions. The experiences described by six subjects in the second study by Blanke were quite different from those reported during a near-death experience and included encounters with strangers, vague impressions of dreaming, feelings of distortion of body movement, and the feeling of being in two positions at once and of viewing only the legs and lower trunk. So how can this piece of research validly refute near-death experiences?

Another alternative proposal is based on a hypothetical phenomenon called DMT dump. During cardiac arrest the pineal gland may react to the perceived threat to the brain by producing a substance called DMT, or N,N-dimethyltryptamine. This is similar to serotonin and has been reported to bring on an extremely intense psychedelic state. The claim is that a near-death experience emerges because of the heightened psychedelic state that the person is in. However, in some other near-death experiences, the brain is not active and therefore the experiences could not have been the result of a psychedelic dump based on the production of DMT.

Some skeptics have suggested that drugs used during resuscitation caused the near-death experiences. This includes ketamine and endogenous chemicals that transmit signals between brain cells. However, professor of medicine Sam Parnia rebutted this by pointing out that no data has been collected from any experimentation to back a possible causal relationship or even an association between neurochemical agents and near-death experiences.[15]

In some near-death experience accounts people accurately reported conversations between others from an out-of-body position. The subjects also experienced all the senses in the near-death experience, including visual, auditory, kinesthetic, and emotional, and had memory recall of it, which cannot be explained through a materialist's perspective.

What is really intriguing is when a subject, who had no prior knowledge of certain people's deaths, reports meeting those people during a near-death experience. One example is from Raymond Moody's book *The Light Beyond*,[16] in the case study of a man who was near death with heart problems at the same time that his sister was near death in a diabetic coma in another part of the same hospital.

The man reported that he left his body and watched the physicians work on him from the corner of the room. Suddenly he found himself conversing with his sister, who was up there with him. When she began to move away from him, he tried to go with her but she told him, "You can't go with me because it's not your time." Then she disappeared into the distance through a tunnel. When he awoke, he told the doctors that his sister had died, but the doctors were not aware of this. At his insistence they discovered that she had indeed just died. Claims of hallucinations and the effects of drug dumps cannot explain this.

Another similar example is the near-death experience of eminent neurosurgeon Eben Alexander. Eben always considered himself a man of science. His belief in evidence-based medicine fueled a career in some of the top institutions in the world. But all that changed on a morning in 2008 when he fell into a coma from a critical case of bacterial meningitis. Scans of his brain revealed massive damage, and he was not expected to survive. However, after his near-death experience his brain went from near total inactivity to an awakened state, which he describes his book *Proof of Heaven: A Neurosurgeon's Journey into the Afterlife*.[17]

He began to move upward fast, and in a flash he went through an opening and found himself in a completely new world, which he describes as "the strangest most beautiful world [he'd] ever seen. Brilliant, vibrant, ecstatic, stunning, and below [him], countryside." He became aware of a glowing beautiful girl next to him who said, "You are loved and cherished, dearly, forever. You have nothing to fear. There is nothing you can do that is wrong." Afterward Eben was of the view that it would take the rest of his life to integrate what he had learned during the experience. Also, the knowledge from it was stored without him memorizing it and was for his good.

After his near-death experience, Eben considered and rejected all the physical explanations of his experience because his neocortex was not functioning at the time of the experience, yet he experienced clarity of vision.

SUMMARY OF CHAPTER 2

For centuries, thousands of people from different cultures and societies and with diverse religious views have had near-death experiences. It seems to happen in around 10 percent of those who have had a life-threatening experience, so they are quite common. They also tend to have a life-changing positive impact on people.

The problem with all the physical explanations of near-death experiences is that some people who have had a near-death experience had a flat EEG at the time, meaning that there was no electrical activity in the cerebral cortex. In addition, if physical states triggered phenomenological experiences then you would expect them to be completely individual. However, the results of near-death experience research show a consistency of experiences, such as communicating with spiritual beings and having a past-life review.

This point and the evidence of rigorous, controlled near-death experience research by medical professionals suggests that consciousness is not contained within the brain and can survive for a short time if not longer after death. Those who have had a near-death experience of expanded consciousness have been given glimpses of the eternal soul and of the afterlife. For most it is a life-changing event that transforms thinking and beliefs in a positive way for a lifetime and brings about a powerful evolution of consciousness.

3
Past Lives

When you realize where you come from you can deal with whatever life brings you, and when death comes you are ready.

LAO-TZU, CHINESE TAOIST MASTER

❖

Ryan began talking about going back home to Hollywood when he was five. He would cry and plead to see his other family. When he was playing at preschool he would often shout, "Action!" and begin to direct imaginary movies. His mother Cyndi went to a local library and picked up some books about Hollywood in the hope it would help Ryan. In one book from a 1932 movie called Night After Night, *Ryan got excited and pointed to one of the men in a photograph and said, "Hey Mama, that's George. We did a picture together. And Mama, that guy's me. I found me."*

With the help of various investigators Ryan's parents discovered that an actor named Marty Martyn had been an extra in Westerns in Hollywood. Many of the details of his story were confirmed, including stars from Hollywood he had met, how he had enjoyed watching surfers on the beach, the type of large house he had lived in, and his favorite food.

This summary of Ryan Hammond's experience can be found in more detail in the book *Return to Life: Extraordinary Cases of Children Who Remember Past Lives*.[1] It was gathered by Jim Tucker, an associate psychiatry professor in the Division of Perceptual Studies at the University of Virginia and appears to be a spontaneous past life recall.

If consciousness does reside outside the body and can survive for a short period after clinical death, as found in near-death experience research, perhaps it can travel from one incarnation to another as in the case of Ryan.

Reincarnation has its roots in the ancient philosophies and religions of India around the second century BCE. In the West, work with past life regression started in the mid-1970s.

CHILDREN'S SPONTANEOUS PAST LIVES

Systematic research of children's past lives first started with Ian Stevenson, an American professor and chairman of the Department of Psychiatry at the University of Virginia. He became intrigued by the cases of children's reported past lives.

He published his first collection of case reports in *Twenty Cases Suggestive of Reincarnation*.[2] He gathered long descriptions of the cases in his efforts to determine precisely what the child had said about a previous life and how well the statements corresponded to the life of the deceased individual. He also investigated if the child could have obtained the information through ordinary means or fraud by doing follow-up visits to check for signs of any personal gains that could account for deception.

His cases came from a wide range of cultures and religions around the world, many from developing countries where the children often lived in isolated villages without media intrusion. In this type of community, they were isolated from many of the variables that could be alternative explanations for reincarnation. A total of 65 fully detailed cases have been published in his books and 260 have been published in articles.

Typical was the case of Kumkum Verma from his book *Cases of the Reincarnation Type*.[3] Kumkum was a girl from a village in India. When she was three and a half years old she began saying that she had lived in Darbhanga, a city of two hundred thousand people that was twenty-five miles away. She named the district of the city where she said she had lived and some of the artisans and craftsmen. Her family did not know anyone from that district, yet Kumkum continued to make numerous statements about it, so her aunt wrote many of them down. Some of her notes were lost, but Stevenson was able to get a copy of eighteen of the statements that her aunt had recorded and were verified. The detail in these statements included her son's name in the life she was describing and the fact that he worked with a hammer, as well as her grandson's name, the town where her father had lived, and many personal details such as having an iron safe at home, a sword hanging near the cot where she slept, and a pet snake that she fed milk to.

Kumkum's father talked to a friend who had an employee from the district in Darbhanga that she had mentioned. He found that a woman had died five years before Kumkum was born and her life matched the details listed above. Of note is that Kumkum's father was a land-owner and homeopathic physician and was not proud that his daughter seemed to remember the life of a blacksmith's wife.

Children's spontaneous past lives like this have a number of similar characteristics. Children start to talk about them between the ages of two and five. The children often express an intense desire to visit the location and family of their previous life and often display behavioral traits completely out of character with their present life but in keeping with their previous one. The past life memories normally relate to the later years of the deceased person's life and in particular their mode of death.[4]

CHILDREN'S SPONTANEOUS PAST LIVES
WITH PHYSICAL MARKS

One case from Stevenson's book *Where Reincarnation and Biology Intersect* is about a little boy from Thailand called Chanai Choomalaiwong.[5] He was born with two birthmarks. One was at the back of his head and was about a quarter of an inch in diameter, and another larger and more irregular one was behind the hairline above his left eye and was about three-quarters of an inch long and a quarter of an inch wide.

When he was three years old, he started saying that he had been a teacher named Bua Kai and that he had been shot on his way to school one day. He begged to be taken to where he said his previous parents lived. There was no autopsy available, so Stevenson talked to Bua Kai's widow, and she said the doctor who examined his body told her that a small round entrance wound at the back of his head and a larger exit wound in front suggested he had been shot from behind. These wounds were consistent with Chanai's birthmarks.

Stevenson was unable to explain why some children have wounds from past lives. In controlled research with reincarnation author Ian Lawton, Andy probed this area and documented it in his book *Exploring the Eternal Soul*.[6] Different groups of evolved spirits of light encountered through ten different subjects in deep trance were asked the same question: "Can physical characteristics be carried over from one life to another?" The following was a typical response:

It generally happens with younger souls who have had a particular emotional trauma involving a primary emotion such as anger, fear, revenge, or pain that has been carried over to the next life. They may have scars or deformations that act as a reminder—although it's not a totally necessary reminder—but it's what that soul has chosen to do. But this goes against what we try and show about letting go. . . . So we try and show them why it is not necessary, but ultimately they have to learn from experience, even if they do things that we may think of as mistakes on the way.

Over the years, Stevenson studied cases in which subjects were born with birthmarks or defects that appeared to match wounds suffered in a past life. He did not want to report any of the cases until he could publish them as a collection. This turned out to be quite a large collection, and in 1997 Stevenson produced *Reincarnation and Biology: A Contribution to the Etiology of Birthmarks and Birth Defects*, a twenty-two-hundred-page, two-volume collection of over two hundred such cases.[7]

Jim Tucker worked with Stevenson for several years before taking over his research upon Stevenson's retirement in 2002. He went on to write the book *Life before Life* with more case studies of children's past life memories.[8] While Ian Stevenson focused on cases in Asia, Tucker studied children in the United States. He developed the strength of case scale that evaluated four aspects of potential cases of reincarnation: whether a physical defect corresponds to the supposed past life, the strength of the statements about the past life, any relevant behaviors that relate to the past life, and an evaluation of the possibility of information coming from the child's current life.[9]

Tucker, Stevenson, and other researchers have studied over twenty-five hundred cases of children's spontaneous past lives, all of which have been scrutinized carefully. So spontaneous recollection of children's past lives is another compelling piece of evidence suggesting consciousness exists outside the physical body.[10]

ADULT PAST LIVES

Past life regression with adults usually involves using light levels of hypnosis trance to help the person to relax their conscious minds. In this state it is easier to access past life memories in their consciousness.

It's typically undertaken in a psychotherapeutic setting to resolve a client's trauma or emotional difficulties in their current life. There is no doubt that many people have had dramatic healing by past life regression therapy, but this does not necessarily prove the past life is real.

Some of the finest confirmed past life cases came from diligent research like that of Australian psychologist Peter Ramster. Peter was initially skeptical about past lives, but the therapeutic results he obtained changed his mind, and he set about checking the historical accuracy of the cases and documented it in his book *The Truth about Reincarnation*.[11]

He conducted an experiment in which he chose three subjects from his home city of Sydney who had particularly vivid recall of past lives in Europe. None of them had ever been to Europe in their current life, so he arranged for them to visit the locations that they had described on the other side of the world to see if the facts could be verified. Independent witnesses and a film crew accompanied them. The results appeared in a television documentary he produced and later in his book *In Search of Lives Past*.[12]

One of the subjects was Gwen McDonald. In a number of sessions in Australia she regressed to the eighteenth-century life of a girl called Rose Duncan who lived with her father, Adam, and his partner, Bessie, in a small cottage not far from Glastonbury, Somerset, UK. When recalling the past life she spoke with an apparent accent and the manner of an uneducated country peasant of that time and place. Rose had run away from an arranged marriage and died of hypothermia at the age of seventeen.

In Sydney, Ramster was able to confirm some details of the past life, such as a named person being an influential landowner in Somerset during that period. More information was confirmed when they traveled to Somerset itself. Gwen led the team to her former home without hesitation or the use of maps. When she came to a road intersection where she said five houses had stood, only one now remained. However, the occupier was able to confirm her story of the other houses, one being a cider house that had been built in 1742 before being pulled down.

Gwen knew correctly the names of villages as they had been two hundred years earlier, even though on modern maps they either did not exist or their names had been changed. She knew local legends in detail, which were confirmed by Somerset historians. Interestingly, Gwen used correctly obscure and obsolete West Country words that are no longer in common use.

Perhaps most stunning of all was that while she was still in Sydney, Gwen described and drew the exterior of the Pilgrims Inn and some carvings on one of several stone floor slabs in the nearby cottage that the owner had stolen from the local abbey. When she led the team (without maps) to the inn that had since been renamed George and the Pilgrim, the exterior was the same as she had drawn it. Even more startling was when they arrived at the nearby cottages described in the past life; they had now become dilapidated chicken sheds. When they swept the floor free of its layers of droppings for the first time in years it revealed the floor slabs from the abbey—and one had carvings exactly as Gwen had drawn it.

In other cases, Ramster mentions subjects being hurt in a past life. One who had been guillotined had a prominent mark across the back of her neck. This has similarities to Stevenson's birthmark and defect cases.

Andy too has had his own experiences of past life regressions to confirm this. One example is a twenty-seven-year-old mother of two girls.[13] Andy first met her when she was a student in one of his training workshops. She had unexplainable pain in her arms and hands so extreme she was not able to pick anything up with her hands and had volunteered to be a demonstration subject. In her past life she had been in charge of an orphanage, and when fire broke out she had desperately tried to save some of the children and burned her hands and arms in the process before dying in the fire.

Another example of diligent historical past life research has been conducted by Reena and detailed in her book *Shrouded Truth*.[14] Over a four-year period, eight clients coming for entirely different reasons spontaneously recalled events in a past life related to the life and times of Jesus. The eight clients were unknown to each other and from different parts of the world. Subsequent sessions with each of them revealed more information, and even those familiar with the Bible were surprised when the information differed from what they expected.

What makes these accounts so interesting is that in a number of areas the past life accounts dovetailed with one another. When they differed from the official Church doctrine they were still backed up by the latest academic research. This included Jesus being married to and having three children with Mary Magdalene, who was not a prostitute but Jesus's chief apostle, and Jesus and Mary spending some time in France. These points are covered in more detail in appendix 2.

XENOGLOSSY

Xenoglossy is the ability of a person to speak a language normally unknown to them while they are experiencing a past life regression. In our experiences this phenomenon only happens occasionally but is quite dramatic when it does. Stevenson had a case study of a thirty-seven-year-old American woman who, under hypnosis, experienced a complete change of voice and personality into those of a male. She spoke in the Swedish language—a language she did not speak or understand when in the normal state of consciousness.[15]

Triona Sheeran, a regression therapist we both know, told us of a fascinating case study from her practice in Ireland:

> I had a client who was a thirty-three-year-old businessman based in Dublin who traveled a lot and other than English could only speak some French, which was learned as a child at school. He came to me after reading a past life book and was inspired about the possibility of learning and gaining wisdom from his previous lives. In particular he wanted to be able to speak Russian so he could converse in that language with a Russian friend.
>
> After taking him into trance I made the intent to take him to a past life in Russia. The first life was around two-hundred years ago, and he was a foot soldier in the army. On returning to his home town, he spent his time in the local tavern while searching for a quiet life, then had a wife and settled down. It was a mundane life although he spent a lot of time conversing with the locals in the tavern. He spoke some Russian phrases during this part of the past life and was comfortable speaking them after the session.
>
> Two weeks later he had another session with the intent of speaking more Russian. He went to a life as a woman with a young boy. It was a simple life living on a farm with no husband but happy to be rearing the child. He spoke more Russian words and phrases throughout this session.
>
> I talked to him five days later, and he confidently said he was speaking passable Russian to his Russian friend with little English involvement and was happy and comfortable in his new abilities. He could not read or write in Russian, just speaking and understanding basic Russian.

What makes xenoglossy interesting is that it is hard to explain away with a materialistic perspective.

ALTERNATIVE VIEWS

One of the arguments against adult past lives being real is that suggestive questions are often used in hypnosis that make a person more likely to have distorted or false memories. Skeptics claim that the source of the past life memories is more likely cryptomnesia and confabulations that combine previous current life experiences, knowledge, and imagination with suggestions from the hypnotist.

So, let's unpack this. Professionally trained past life therapists ask open questions such as "What happens next?" or "Tell me more about . . ." or "What is being communicated to you?" and closed questions such as, "Has your heart stopped beating?" at the past life death point to confirm information. In the case of Peter Ramster's and Reena's subjects, the past life regressions revealed amazing information that the person had no prior knowledge of that was corroborated with diligent research before publication.

Another one of the arguments against past lives being real is the factor of imagination—that people have just imagined these lives. In Reena's research, how could the subjects have imagined the accounts of Jesus's time without being biblical scholars? It is also very common for emotions and physical sensations consistent with the past life to emerge, and this is highly unlikely to happen with a story from the imagination.

We have also worked with Maria Consuelo Valentini, a neurologist, radiologist, and chief of the Department of Neuroradiology at Città della Salute e della Scienza in Turin, Italy.[16] She and her team used two different MRI scanners in two different hospitals to monitor the brain imaging of two different subjects, one male and one female of different hypnotic ability and beliefs. First the subjects were asked to recall a real current life memory, then an imaginary memory, and then they were given a past life regression. Analysis of the images found that during the past life experience there was no activation of the brain area used for storing current life memories or imagination. The part of the brain that was activated was associated with deep relaxation or transpersonal experiences. This suggests that past life memories cannot derive from imagination or previous current life memories.

Sometimes the details given in past life accounts do not always correspond to later research. However, if someone wrongly recalls a memory of their childhood, does this mean that all their childhood memories are unreal? Likewise, if a detail in the past life is wrong, does that mean all the past life memories are wrong? Also, who is to say that the research is more accurate than the past life story? Historical research is normally based on intelligent deductions of physical evidence found and stories told at the time. However, deductions do not make an absolute truth, especially when new physical evidence is found all the time that changes the historical narrative.

Psychologically speaking, what we experience is a matter of perception. We mostly retain the perception that has had the biggest impact on us. For example, suppose two people go to a Formula 1 Grand Prix. The strongest impressions one person may have could be of the loud sounds every time the cars drive past and the searing heat. If you asked them about details later, they may not be able to remember the color of the cars or the names of drivers. Another person who has a background in engineering may be more interested in the speed, corner turns, and horsepower of the cars. If you asked them afterward, they may not remember the heat, pollution, and loud noises but would give an enthusiastic monologue about the details and mechanics of the cars.

In 1916, Carl Jung introduced the concept of the collective unconscious in his essay "The Structure of the Unconscious." This is an idea that we all share a common consciousness that includes past lives, and we can all tap into it. Some skeptics have suggested that people somehow tap into this collective experience rather than one of their own past lives. However, as a general rule it is very difficult to create an emotional reaction from the collective unconscious. It's almost like having an emotional reaction from watching a scene in a movie versus actually experiencing the emotional event in person. The more intense the emotion and body sensations, the more likely it is to be a real past life memory.

One criticism of children's spontaneous past lives is the relatively haphazard way in which reports of cases arrived to Stevenson, often many years later, and that fraud may be involved. However, Stevenson's research methods were deliberately designed to reveal this. Also, there was little motive for fraud as many of the children were from small villages in Asia where mistruths dishonor the community, and in some cases the recollections of past lives placed the children in positions of rejection by the family. And fraud does not explain the unusual behavior traits and phobias displayed by a great number of child subjects or the birthmarks or other physical birth defects that were found to correspond to the death wounds of the deceased person.

SUMMARY OF CHAPTER 3

Hundreds of thousands of adults have experienced past lives. When the past life information is methodically gathered and verified by academic, historical, and personal current life corroboration, it becomes a persuasive piece of evidence. Many of these past life accounts are of nonfamous, simple-living folk, yet at times they are deeply emotional. The person being regressed cries, laughs, shivers, and screams during their sessions. Over the years, twenty-five hundred children have had their spontaneous past life recollections rigorously investigated, and many of the details have been confirmed by the researchers.

The materialist view of consciousness is that the awareness stays with the body—either within the brain or within the physical matter of the body. If this is true, how are people able to transcend time with verifiable information, the associated emotions, and occasionally the physical marks of the past lives if the memories, awareness, and emotions perish with the past life body and brain?

If consciousness survives after permanent bodily death, then like near-death experiences, these past life recollections by children and adults can be attributed to the fact that they are accessing or tapping into their wider consciousness. And it this ability to expand consciousness that this book is focused on.

4
Between Lives Spiritual Regression

Out beyond ideas of wrongdoing and right doing,
There is a field. I'll meet you there.
Jalal al-Din Rumi, thirteenth-century Sufi

---◈---

I feel as though I'm lifting. God, my body is in a mess. It's just lying in the mud, where it was hit. I can't move on yet. I'm just taking in all this carnage. It's terrible. What purpose? The pain's stopped though. Thank goodness. No pain. No pain! Just stillness and quiet, and it's a pleasant feeling really. I just want to watch what they do with the body. It's put on a stretcher. Somebody's fiddling around with it and they take it away. There is a big trench, and they are throwing us all in. Half a dozen of us, and they just bury us. It's the end, isn't it? That's it . . . I just see little lights in the distance. I'm just getting energized. It's like someone plugging me into the electricity. Plugging me into some energy. It's a nice feeling and I don't want to leave. . . . A rest, they call it, but this can't be rest. It's lovely!

The preceding account is from one of Andy's clients, who we will call John. He is describing his past life death as a First World War soldier.[1] John's account goes beyond the past life death and describes looking down at his dead body and the energetic help he experiences to overcome the traumatic death.

John's feedback after the session was "Life was exceedingly difficult for me and I propounded the theory that the individual was better off having not been born, thereby being excused from the 'sufferings' of life. I am a person who needs to know 'the detail' and 'the why' and the experience was a huge leap forward in my spiritual growth."

This is a short extract of his session. A full one navigates all the memories and experiences between lives and is something anyone can experience to provide profound insights about who they really are at a soul level. It provides an expansion of consciousness that in John's case led to a transformation in his life.

PIONEERS OF BETWEEN LIVES REGRESSION

One of the first pioneers of between lives regression was Edith Fiore. She received her doctorate in psychology from the University of Miami. In the 1970s she began to amass between lives material that was published in her book *You Have Been Here Before*, published in 1979.[2]

In the following decade, Peter Ramster, while working with past lives, discovered the soul memories between lives by chance when he used an imprecise command. He incorporated his finding in 1980 in his book *The Truth about Reincarnation*.[3]

A similar experience happened with Canadian psychiatrist Joel Whitton. He instructed a client in a past life to go back to the life before the one she was in and was amazed to find her describing herself as being "in the sky . . . waiting to be born . . . watching my mother." Joel went on to make a huge contribution to the understanding of the between life experience by deliberately investigating the phenomenon with a number of his more responsive subjects, publishing his research in his 1986 collaboration with Joe Fisher in their book *Life Between Life*.[4]

Dolores Cannon wrote several past life books and made a contribution to spiritual life between lives in 1993 in her book *Between Death and Life*[5] followed by psychiatrist Shakuntala Modi in her 1997 book, *Remarkable Healings*.[6]

The most successful pioneer to bring this to public consciousness was American Michael Newton with what he called *Life between Lives*. Like many of the others working in this area he was skeptical about reincarnation and stumbled upon the soul memories while working with past life regression. From that point on he concentrated most of his efforts on investigating this area as thoroughly as he could, publishing his findings based on thousands of cases in his books *Journey of Souls*[7] and *Destiny of Souls*[8] in 1994 and 2000 respectively.

Andy was trained by Michael and worked with him before offering what he calls between lives spiritual regression training to therapists, and then went on to take his work further himself. In 2006, with the help of researcher and author Ian Lawton, *Exploring the Eternal Soul*[9] was published. This book gathered information from case studies that added to the between lives process in great detail, and it analyzed the pioneers' research to demonstrate the consistency of key events. The following sections provide a summary of these events.

KEY EVENTS OF A BETWEEN LIVES
SPIRITUAL REGRESSION

For this a client needs to be in a deep level of trance. At this level the client's conscious mind is inactive, and their intuition link opens fully to the between lives memories. The normal way of entering between life memories is from a past life while the client is in deep hypnosis. There is a fluidity to the order of the events and not all are experienced by everyone. However, there is always a transition between leaving the physical body and reincarnating into the baby in the next life. Also, a past life review needs to take place before any planning occurs for the next life.

Transition via a Tunnel or Light

A transition happens after the past life death, and the therapist ensures death has occurred by asking the subject if their heart has stopped beating and then what happens next. The client usually expresses a sudden sense of lightness and freedom, and sometimes the death scene is observed for a while with an air of detachment. The previous case study on John illustrates this. Sometimes a tunnel is mentioned but more often they are drawn to a light. The light, on closer examination, normally turns out to be one or more welcoming souls. Most clients talk of being pulled by unseen forces toward this light.

Meeting with Friends, Family, or Spirit Guides

Meeting with spiritual beings is often part of the transition. These beings may be deceased people known from that life, possibly loved ones, or the client's spirit guides. A spirit guide is a spiritual being involved with another soul's life plan who oversees the incarnation to provide guidance. An important principle in the spirit realms is that energy follows thought. This allows spirit beings to change their appearance from multicolored soul energy into a human or semihuman shape to make the incoming soul more at ease.

Varied Perception of Surroundings

All of the between lives pioneers report that souls can give their surroundings varying amounts of semiphysical form in the spirit plane using the energy-follows-thought principle. It often happens during the initial transition, particularly for less experienced souls that need physical characteristics to make them feel more comfortable and at home. Sometimes the settings are described as classrooms and libraries or perceived as temples with domes and columns, crystalline castles, or green meadows and flowers. These characteristics often contain elements of a favorite building or scene from the life on Earth.

Initial Rest and Energy Restoring

Consciousness, after leaving the physical body, still carries unresolved negative emotions from the life. Clearing this emotional energy as soon as possible is important for the journey to the higher vibration levels of the spirit realms. There is a similarity and overlap between resting and healing, and more traumatized souls may also need an extra period of rest and recuperation between energy healing sessions. The level of healing depends on the challenges of the life and the level of maturity of the soul.

Healing Shower of Energy

Another way healing can be experienced is through a process that is similar to a shower. Energy healing this way is done gradually, particularly for more traumatized souls. Often a past life review is done between each emotional layer removed. Newton suggests the healing process is far more intensive for souls who have had more traumatic lives. He describes what appears to be a sort of emergency treatment center for seriously traumatized souls. Here they are reshaped or even remodeled via transfusions of pure, new soul energy.

Soul Groups

We all have a group of souls we work closely with in varied relationships over many lives, and the reunion with them is always a profoundly moving experience. The primary aim of all souls is to learn, experience, and grow.

So, time with the soul group is often characterized by discussions about shared lives, what was handled well and what could have been handled better. In this context the ability to replay and role-play events is helpful. Occasionally souls move to a different soul group to work on new lessons.

Past Life Review

An important event is a review of the last life. This can be a solitary process done alone if the soul is more experienced, or it can be aided by the spirit guide because they have overseen the life and know the soul's learning objectives. Sometimes a life review can be done with the guidance of evolved light beings, often called Elders, who have mastered the reincarnation process and can offer deeper insights.

Replay/Role-Play via Life Books and Films

Some people describe past life reviews taking place in a library environment in which the books in front of them come alive like a film. Others say that they can enter the film to replay various events or even to role-play them by doing things differently and seeing what happens. And some report that they can place themselves in the bodies of others to feel exactly what effect their actions had on them.

Ongoing Classroom Learning

Souls talk about intellectual studies in vast halls of learning equipped with libraries and seminar rooms. Within them some souls learn to be doctors and lawyers and study their respective disciplines, while other souls apply themselves to subjects such as the laws of the universe and other metaphysical topics.

Nonjudgmental Nature of Reviews

During past life reviews the only judgment comes from the soul itself and not from the more experienced souls that might be assisting.

This is because the soul perspective is totally unlike the human perceptive and cannot include self-deception or excuses. All the actions, and even more important the intentions, are laid bare. And it is up to the soul, aided by spirit guides and Elders, to cope with the reaction to them.

Next-Life Planning

At some point next-life planning takes place. While it is done in an energy setting, a human type form such as a dome and walls can be projected to create the impression of a place of importance. The face projected by the Elders also has a meaning, perhaps to make the soul more at ease. Planning normally involves an awareness of who the parents will be, where they live, their circumstances, and what sex they will be. Many people reveal that they receive a fuller preview, often describing it as being similar to seeing a film that they can stop, rewind, fast-forward, and even enter to fully experience what is going on.

Planning is probably the most crucial aspect of the between lives experience because it indicates that souls have complete control and personal responsibility for the new life. Any life previews only represent major probabilities so lives are not completely predetermined, and some deviation may occur when souls use free will.

Choice to Reject the Life Plan Offered

If a soul is given only one life option, and it is not attractive, they may initially reject the idea. It might be assumed that souls can be forced into a life they do not want. Further probing always confirms that this is not the case, and they can turn it down. What actually happens is that less-experienced souls usually take a little time to appreciate that this is what they need, if they are to make any proper progress to break free from repetitive patterns of behavior.

Multiple Life Plans Offered

Sometimes souls may be given a preview of several different lives and asked to choose which one they think will be of most use for learning and growth. Spirit guides and Elders are on hand to provide assistance and advice. Often plans are discussed with other soul group members who will be involved in that life, and they may even agree on triggers that will help recognize them when in physical bodies.

Training in Specialization

For most souls the time between lives is spent preparing to manage future emotional issues or difficult situations not mastered in a previous life. For more evolved souls, time can also be spent learning new skills such as healing with energy, energy manipulation, or even learning to be spirit guides.

Incarnation

Incarnation involves entering the baby while it is still in the womb, which can be any time from the point of conception to just before birth. The process of merging the soul with the new physical body is gradual and sometimes difficult, involving matching the individual pattern and frequency of soul energy to that of the developing brain. The stress of this process is often reduced by floating out of the body for short periods.

Another aspect of the return to the earth plane is the gradual weakening of the incarnating soul connection to the spirit realms and the gradual lowering of the veil of amnesia. The reason for this is that if souls knew all about their life plans in advance, it would be like taking an exam with all the answers, and no real learning would occur. Also, if souls remembered too much about the bliss of the spirit realms after incarnation, they would be constantly homesick and long to return. This explains why children often have spontaneous past life recall more often than adults.

The following table shows which of the major events occurring between lives have been covered in each of the early pioneers' books.[10]

Event	Tomlinson	Newton	Ramster	Whitton	Cannon	Modi	Fiore
Transition via a tunnel or light	X	X	X	X	X	X	X
Meeting with friends, family, or spirit guides	X	X	X	X	X	X	X
Varied perception of surroundings	X	X		X	X		
Initial rest and energy restoring	X	X	X			X	
Healing shower of energy	X	X			X	X	
Soul groups	X	X	X	X	X	X	
Past life review	X	X		X	X	X	X
Replay/role-play via life books and films	X	X	X	X	X	X	
Ongoing classroom learning	X	X	X	X	X	X	
Nonjudgmental nature of reviews	X	X	X	X	X	X	X
Next-life planning	X	X	X	X	X	X	X
Choice to reject the life plan offered	X	X	X	X	X	X	X
Multiple life plans offered	X	X	X				
Training in specialization	X	X		X	X		

Some of the differences in the table can be accounted for by the fact that many of the early pioneers were self-taught, so their skills in navigating the between lives experience were still developing. Also, some of the early pioneers only used a limited number of subjects.

Although the elements described above provide a consistent underlying thread, they are not all experienced by every subject during every between lives session. Sometimes the emphasis may be more on review or on planning or on meeting soul groups. This does not necessarily mean that each of the key elements is not experienced during the between lives period. But when people are recalling the soul experience in human form, some things may be more important than others, and the order of the key events may vary.

IMPACT OF BETWEEN LIVES
SPIRITUAL REGRESSION

Although I feel that my words cannot do it justice, this was for me an extremely profound experience. It put a lot of "issues" in my life into context and enabled me to look at the bigger picture in terms of the journey of my energetic soul. I can only say thank you to the universe for making this opportunity available, for giving me this glimpse of my soul, my life between lives. It was a magical, wonderful, and humbling experience. It has touched me, changed my view on life, and opened up my eyes, my heart, and my soul to a greater calm. I have understanding, love, and respect for life, for others on their journeys, for the universe, and for myself.

The above quote is what Veronica Perry said about her between lives spiritual regression in Andy's book *Exploring the Eternal Soul*.[11]

Based on the research that Andy and Ian Lawton did with fifteen subjects, the following are the impacts these sessions had on their lives:[12]

+ No longer having a fear of death
+ Being able to see the spiritual perspective to improve difficult relationships
+ Having a positive attitude about the future
+ Having more understanding, love, and respect for life and others
+ Leading a more positive life
+ Having a greater sensitivity for how personal decisions impact others
+ Knowing that they are following their soul's life purpose

ALTERNATIVE VIEWS

Some opponents have suggested that the consistency of the between lives experiences reported by the pioneers' subjects resulted because they had specific belief systems or prior knowledge or that the pioneers engaged in undue subjective leading.

As to subjects having prior knowledge of the between lives period itself, this is highly unlikely to have occurred on any significant scale. Most of the pioneers' books were not even close to being bestsellers at the time, and their work was done quite independently. A possible exception was Michael Newton, whose first publication did not come out until long after most of the other pioneering work had been published. And throughout his own studies, Andy carefully screened out any subjects that had any prior knowledge.

The possibility of the pioneers potentially leading their subjects is far less common than skeptics may assume. Based on our experience, clients under deep hypnosis take instructions extremely literally, much like a computer program. So at the very least, deliberate falsification of information is virtually impossible unless the person is not really in trance, and a skilled therapist can tell when that is the case. For the same reason, people cannot just be told to experience something because for the most part they have to be actually having the experience to report on it. Many of the transcripts of between lives sessions are now available and reveal that the authors were mainly asking open questions and not making leading suggestions.

SUMMARY OF CHAPTER 4

Thousands of people have now had their own between lives experience guided by the pioneers or other between lives therapists trained by them. The between lives reports show a remarkable consistency, but what is particularly important is that many of the people in these between lives spiritual regressions had no prior knowledge that any experience existed between lives.

They also had beliefs ranging from atheism to all the world's major religions. This is an important point to note: the clients' previous beliefs seem to make no difference in the nature of their between lives experience. This leads to the question, Are between life regressions and near-death experiences similar in any way? This will be the focus of the next chapter.

At the end of the day, there is no materialist or scientific research that conclusively proves consciousness is only contained in the physical brain and that the eternal soul does not exist. However, there are plenty of valid, credible, and consistent processes and studies of the time between lives that have established the survival of our consciousness, referred to as our eternal soul, and its journey between lives.

5

Comparison of Near-Death Experiences and Between Lives Spiritual Regressions

Greet Yourself In your thousand other forms as you mount the hidden tide and travel back home.

HAFIZ, FOURTEENTH-CENTURY
PERSIAN MYSTIC AND POET

————————— ◇ —————————

*I was in a tunnel, traveling at enormous speed toward a light. . . .
The walls . . . were a blur . . . There was tremendous sound, too . . .*

*I was suddenly frightened. I had no idea where I was bound at
such speed, nor had anything in my life prepared me for this adventure.
As soon as I realized I was afraid, a presence reached out to me;
not physically, but telepathically. It was a calming, gentle presence
and a voice which said, "Take it easy. Everything is OK. Relax," and
this thought immediately induced a soothing effect on me, far more
powerful than anything within the experience of my stressful life. . . .*

I arrived at a library. It was a vast old traditional building, containing all of the wisdom of the ages, everything ever said or written. Room upon room, shelf upon shelf of books stretched away as far as the eye could see. . . . My guide, for by now I thought of him as such, told me I must study and learn from the infinite array of wisdom before us. I was dismayed, and said there was no way I was capable of such a task. . . .

My guide told me plainly that it was time for me to go . . . I protested, saying the circumstances of my life were such that I could not continue . . . I was asked to be more specific, and I recalled an area of my life in which I had experienced difficulty. Instantly I was filled with an overpowering sense of that specific emotion. It was almost unbearable. Then, with no more than a gesture, the pain was made to vanish, to be replaced by a glorious sense of well-being and love. This process was repeated several times, with specific areas of my life where I had been experiencing difficulty. My friend then pointed out that I could perform this astonishing feat myself. It was not at all difficult, he said, and I would have an opportunity during the balance of my life to practice and to make a beginning learning about some of the other things I had experienced during this journey.

The preceding extract detailed Bob Helm's near-death experience and was published by Kenneth Ring in the *Journal of Near-Death Studies*.[1] Bob worked for Canadian television, and his near-death experience happened during an operation to repair a broken leg after an automobile accident. We move now to an excerpt of the between lives spiritual regression account of one of Andy's clients we can call Sue:

It's over, I don't know what happens next, but it's all gone black. . . . I'm hovering over the whole thing. I'm looking down on it all feeling so sad. . . . Something's pulling me upward. I feel as if there are two light energies lifting me up. They don't have form, but they feel wonderfully supportive. It's like they're through a round door. . . . Whatever it is has created a sea of blue, beautiful, everything is blue and as I move through this blue, something happens to my own light field. . . . It permeates all through me. . . . It feels like all those things that were stuck to me just float away. It's like being in an indigo-blue bath of gentle releasing light. I can't describe it, and I just float in this sea of blue . . . it's like going to sleep. And everything just floats off me and I start to change form . . . all those memories of that battlefield just float away. . . .

I've moved on. . . . It has an energetic structure, it's not a hall or a room, it's like a field or an orb. It's as if I'm passing through this field, and I must meet these colored energies. . . . I feel quite vulnerable in front of them. I don't feel there's judgment or criticism, but it's as if their energies, each one directs theirs . . . it's like a laser with the frequency of the different colors from each of them. . . . Then a kind of film. . . . I was safe in my skin until I went to war in that lifetime. I didn't have a problem with being in my body before and after my sexuality hadn't really flowered. . . . I was the man of the family and I misused my power . . . [deep sigh] so the yellow hue . . . restores the balance and the heart . . . each one of them in turn are rebalancing of the whole soul's energetic, which is linked with energy centers. . . . This is a kind of restructuring of the soul.

Even though the information came through two different processes, there are many similarities between Bob's and Sue's experiences. Both give accounts of leaving the body, seeing lights of various colors, experiencing some sort of healing, meeting spiritual people, and having a life review.

OUR LARGE-SCALE RESEARCH

We decided to take the comparison further using the work of Kenneth Ring, Pim van Lommel, Bruce Greyson and British neuropsychiatrist Peter Fenwick who researched near-death experiences and published it in his books *The Truth in the Light*[2] and *The Art of Dying*.[3] For completeness we also included the results from Gallup.

Between them they reviewed 586 near-death experience subjects using sets of questions they had each created about the near-death experience. However, there is nothing comparing the near-death experience to the between lives spiritual regression. So, to perform a strong comparison, we set about doing more research into between lives spiritual regression experiences.

Between us, we have been training therapists to carry out between lives spiritual regression internationally for nearly twenty years through the Past Life Regression Academy.[4] To qualify, therapists need to submit five between lives spiritual regression case studies for final certification. The case studies are done to a standardized template that requires information to be provided for each of the between lives spiritual regression stages, and detailing what the client gains immediately after the session.[5]

When we analyzed this information, we realized there were 537 different subject case studies from the work of 108 therapists we had trained. This gave us a solid foundation that we could work with.

In comparing between lives spiritual regression cases with near-death experience research, we acknowledge that a major obvious difference between them is that in the between lives the therapist guides the session, while the near-death experience evolves in a spontaneous way. For example, therapists start the regression from a client's last past life and ensure that the heart had stopped in that life before continuing with the regression. As the client moves out of the body unprompted, they may be asked about what they are aware of, which accounts for them knowing they are out of the body.

The near-death experience only covers the early stages of a between lives spiritual regression because the experience is stopped to return to the current life. So for a comparison, just the following five stages of the process have been used:

1. Out of body/transition via a tunnel or light
2. Meeting with friends, family, or spirit guides
3. Varied perception of surroundings
4. Initial rest and energy restoring
5. Past life review (possibly through replay/role-play via life books and films)

RESEARCH COMPARISON BETWEEN NEAR-DEATH EXPERIENCE AND BETWEEN LIVES SPIRITUAL REGRESSION

The figure below is a visual representation of the timeline that we will look at in this section. It covers the past life (PL), the between lives spiritual regression (BLSR), the current life (CL), and the near-death experience (NDE).

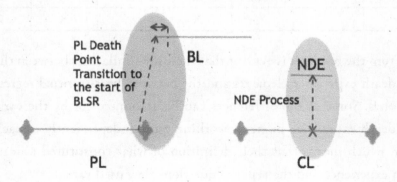

Visual Representation of the NDE and BLSR

The between lives spiritual regression (BLSR in the table) findings of the research come from the 537 cases involving people all around the world that were collected over twenty years. They are summarized and compared to the findings in the near-death experience (NDE) research in the table below. More detailed results are covered in appendix 1.

Stage	NDE Ring (102 subjects)	NDE Gallup (number of subjects unknown)	NDE Greyson (74 subjects)	NDE van Lommel (62 subjects)	NDE Fenwick (300 subjects)	BLSR AT & RK (537 subjects)
Out-of-body experience	X	X	X	X	X	X
Visual perception	X	X	X	X	X	X
Audible sounds or voices	X	X	X		X	X
Positive emotions	X	X	X	X	X	X
Light phenomena	X	X	X		X	X
Moving through a tunnel or darkness	X	X	X	X	X	X
Communication with other beings	X	X	X	X		X
Another world or celestial landscape		X	X	X	X	X
Meeting deceased persons			X	X	X	X
Life review	X	X	X	X	X	X
Precognition		X	X		X	X

From the results it is evident that there are similarities between the near-death experience elements and the between lives spiritual regression ones. Some of the differences can be accounted for by the early near-death experience pioneers working quite independently of each other, which means that their definition of what constituted a near-death experience and the types of questions they used varied.

Also, many people cannot put the near-death experience into words, so they use metaphors that cannot be taken literally. Their cultural background can also affect the experience. For example, people in the West may use the word *tunnel* while people in Africa, where few tunnels exist, may use the word *cave*. So the questions asked to understand the experience need to take this into account.

Turning to some of the more subtle differences observed, very few between lives spiritual regression experiences had accounts of tunnels, which were more common with near-death experiences. Between lives spiritual regression was more about seeing lights or being drawn toward them. Perhaps the tunnel was in place to energetically guide the person's consciousness in a near-death experience to ensure it safely returned to the body.

Unexpectedly, there are significantly fewer accounts of positive emotions in the between lives spiritual regression accounts than in the near-death experience accounts. Many near-death experience subjects reported feeling joy and peace, being one with everything, and receiving unconditional love from a divine being. This may have similarities with the healing stage of between lives sessions where the old emotions are stripped off leaving positive emotions. Perhaps our therapists do not ask enough questions in this stage to ascertain the emotions.

The between lives spiritual regression accounts have a significantly higher number of life reviews than the near-death experience accounts. They also experience them in great detail. This is because the therapists are trained to ask many questions in this area to set the client's understanding for the later planning stages. Also, prior to a session, clients are screened to ensure they will be open to this learning should it emerge, while in a near-death experience, there is no deliberate screening process.

Those who have had a near-death experience reported that time appears to be nonexistent, with everything happening all at once. This has similarities with between lives spiritual regression experiences.[6]

COMPARISON OF THE IMPACTS FOLLOWING THESE EXPERIENCES

Not all the near-death pioneers collected information on the near-death impact years after the event. Also, the between lives spiritual regression case studies did not collect that information either. So we turned to the research that Andy and Ian Lawton did with fifteen between lives spiritual regression subjects, which had this information, and compared it with the experiences of those near-death researchers who included long-term impact on their questionnaires.

The following table shows the similarities of impact. The main areas of difference are shown in the last four rows. Those seeking a between lives spiritual regression often already had a previous interest in intuitive and spiritual aspects, while those with a near-death experience often had a previous materialist view of the world.

Impact	BLSR Tomlinson	NDE Ring	NDE Greyson	NDE van Lommel
No longer having a fear of death	X	X	X	X
Becoming less suicidal			X	
Being able to see the spiritual perspective to improve difficult relationships	X			X
Having a positive attitude about the future and a sense of well-being and appreciating life	X	X	X	X
Having more understanding, love, and respect for life and others	X	X		X

Impact	BLSR	NDE	NDE	NDE
	Tomlinson	Ring	Greyson	van Lommel
Leading a more positive life and understanding how personal decisions impact others	X			X
Knowing that they are following their soul's life purpose or spiritual well-being	X	X	X	X
Having less concern about acquiring material wealth		X	X	X
Having a greater desire to learn		X		
Becoming more intuitive		X		X
Experiencing a renewed interest in religion or spirituality		X	X	X

VERIFICATION

To understand the comparison in more detail we decided to find subjects who had experienced both and compare them. Although the study was limited to two people plus Reena's experience, it does provide some interesting insights.

When Reena shared her near-death experience in a webinar to graduates of the Past Life Regression Academy, she mentioned her insight about the similarity between her near-death experience and her between lives spiritual regression. Two attendees also had both contacted her to share their experiences. The first person was Anita Das:

When my near-death experience started my crown spontaneously burst open and I initially saw my body below me before traveling up the tube. I noticed that I could see everything perfectly, even without wearing my glasses, and that everything was so clear and vibrant. I felt so free and expansive as though I had been restricted by the physical body. I then traveled up the tube. I was lifted upward through my crown upstream in what felt like an extremely fast current of water propelling me upward like a water slide tube that was flowing upward instead of down. I was consciously traveling up as opposed to a sense of me traveling up. It was like being pulled by a rapid and powerful current that I was powerless to resist. I was fully conscious and aware of everything around me and all that I was experiencing in real time. I felt total freedom and expansion of being beyond anything I'd ever experienced. As I was engulfed in bright light, I felt infinitely loved, supported and a tremendous expansiveness of being, knowing and perceiving.

After my near-death experience I was able to naturally be a trance medium or voice channel and channel light beings as an out-of-body channel. I noticed that I was able to see past lives of clients where they needed healing, watching the past life scenes as though a virtual video was playing, and felt that I had brought back more spiritual energy and had these past life healing and energy healing abilities, which I did not have before.

My experience and perspective of life completely changed after the near-death experience, in that I lived in a state of flow and followed breadcrumbs and synchronicities which led me to train in a number of spiritual healing and therapy modalities. Whereas before I had to work to make things happen, I felt I flowed more with life and everything came to me effortlessly, and I was able to manifest just through my thoughts, and I was able to see and feel people's energy. I was much more aware of the beauty of nature and could easily spend hours just appreciating the beauty of nature; for example, just watching the tree sway in the wind. I also noticed a change in my breathing that was slower and deeper and felt a great sense of calm and deep inner peace.

I was given the choice to leave or come back. As soon as I made the choice to come back, I was brought back down into my body.

It was as if I could communicate telepathically through my thoughts and had no need to use words. I felt that I had a connection with everyone I met after the near-death experience in that it was reconnecting me to old-soul and past-life connections. I also had a greater sense of my soul purpose or mission and felt more driven at a soul level to be of service through healing and teaching, and appreciated the unity, oneness, and connection to all beings; the importance of the present moment and the serenity, stillness, and inner peace of just being.

Anita had experienced two between lives spiritual regression sessions after the near-death experience and thought that they would have been different if they had happened first. She felt that the near-death experience had the most impact, but the between lives sessions were useful in providing validation that she was following her soul purpose. The second between lives spiritual regression session served to provide greater insights and connection with her authentic aspects and explained why throughout her life she had never felt that she truly belonged here. It also provided meaning to the various spiritual experiences, downloads, and updates that had been transmitted to her over the years. While her sessions seemed very validating and life-affirming, her near-death experience seemed to be a major turning point in her life.

The second person who shared her experience with Reena—we will call her Ingrid Court—had a distressing near-death experience and after that had a between lives spiritual regression.

I started getting multiple panic attacks daily, a situation that went on for about six months. I couldn't leave my apartment anymore, I just lay in bed crippled with fear and desperation. Sometime then I stopped eating, my body couldn't swallow food anymore, not even drink water.

After a few days of that, I went to lie down on my bed and gradually stopped moving. It was a weird catatonic state that went on for ten hours, then twelve and into the night. I couldn't move a muscle and suddenly felt there was no fear left in my body. It felt like a darkness, a nothingness had taken its place. I wondered if I was experiencing disassociation, but it felt different than other times I had felt that. I was not aware of any pain, I just perceived my body as something heavy, that I could just leave on the bed. I had a sense or a thought, I can't remember which, that this is the night when I get to decide if I stay, or I go.

I suddenly felt so much clarity, which for a malnourished, mentally ill person who had been sleeping one to two hours at night for the past six months was quite remarkable. I was more than clear; I was alert. I remember wondering what I was going to choose, wondering how long it would take for my family to find me. Apparently, I stayed in that experience for about eighteen hours, but time did not register like that for me. I did not see any light, or have feelings of hope or joy, but I was able to get a reprieve from the unbearably turbulent experience that my life had become. And then I chose. I made an agreement with God. If an opportunity to live came, I would take it. Two hours later I received the call that saved my life.

I never quite thought of that transformational experience as a near-death experience because I had not seen a light or angels or the other "usuals" that people seem to report. Until one day when I had my between lives session, and it all started with that familiar darkness. There was nothing or no one there, and I was just waiting in my body trying to figure out, What now? And then I started to remember, Oh, I need to rise, it always takes me a while to figure it out.

As I moved through the experience, I learned a lot more about the other realm and my life that I could summarize here, but it all felt colder and more mental than what I now call my near-death experience. It all felt interesting and clarified certain questions I had, but it didn't shake me to my core, the way that the other experience had.

I had been on my "death bed" quite a few times previously, one time even in the hospital, but it never felt risky, it never felt believable. This had been something different that registered as a before and after in my life. From then on, I started attracting only spiritual people in my life who also helped expose me to the spiritual therapies that would completely change my existence. A year later I left my profession and dedicated myself to becoming a spiritual healer. One little skill that I seem to have picked up along the way is the ability to know when someone is about to leave the planet. I have become quite comfortable walking the line that separates our two existences.

Before sharing her experiences with us, Ingrid started off by saying that her near-death experience was vivid, and her between lives spiritual regression was murky. Unlike her near-death experience, which created clear shifts in her life, she said that her between lives was abstract, and she found it difficult to translate it into practical terms. However, she said that the session provided clarity for the birth of her first child and the passing away of her grandfather.

In her session she had information about her children and received an image of her grandfather turning into a baby and falling into her hands. So, in real life when her grandfather died, she felt like she was able to cope with his death. When her child was born a month later, she felt a strong connection between her son and her grandpa.

The other aspect that she received clarity on was pursuing her teaching profession. The near-death experience helped her let go of her previous profession, and the between lives spiritual regression gave her a direction to focus on moving forward.

DIFFERENCES

The first difference between Anita, Ingrid, and Reena's experiences was that the near-death experience came as a complete surprise. None of them were expecting it, so it took time during and after the experience to come to terms with exactly what was happening and what had happened. With the between lives spiritual regression, naturally they were aware that they were going to have the experience. The emotions of having a between lives experience were ones of excitement and anticipation.

The second major difference is that some near-death experiences can be distressing. The report of Ingrid Court was of intense fear and everything being black: "Just dark as I felt my consciousness splitting from my body. It was like one part of me was poisoned, and the other part was set free." When she had her between lives spiritual regression the visual experience was similar except for the absence of fear, because she knew it would not be the end of her current life.

All acknowledged that while both experiences were vivid, the difference was that in a between lives session, one was reliving a past memory, and in a near-death experience one was undergoing something in real time. As Anita said,

> During the between lives spiritual regression, I sensed, saw, felt, heard everything very clearly, but a part of me was still aware that my instrument was on the earth plane. It felt more like reliving or recalling a vivid memory, whereas in the near-death experience I was consciously experiencing the expansion and vastness of my essence with full conscious awareness in the Now moment rather than remembering or reliving a vivid memory.

DISTRESSING NEAR-DEATH EXPERIENCES

The biggest difference between the two types of experience is that some near-death experiences can be distressing as Ingrid encountered. Nancy Evans Bush, in her book *Dancing Past the Dark*, has an account of Lou, who was forty-eight and despondent over the persistent disappointments in his life.

> *From the roof of the utility shed in my back yard I jumped to the ground. Luckily for me I had forgotten the broken lawn chair that lay near the shed. My feet hit the chair and broke my fall, or my neck would have been broken. I hung in the rope and strangled.*
>
> *I was outside my physical body. I saw my body hanging in the rope; it looked awful. I was terrified, could see and hear but different—hard to explain. Demons were all around me. I could hear them but could not see them. They chattered like blackbirds. It was as if they knew they had me and had all eternity to drag me down into hell, to torment me. It would have been the worst kind of hell, trapped hopeless between two worlds, wandering lost and confused for all eternity.*
>
> *I had to get back into my body. Oh my God, I needed help. I ran to the house, went in through the door without opening it, cried out to my wife but she could not hear me, so I went right into her body. I could see and hear with her eyes and ears. Then I made contact, heard her say, "Oh, my God!"*
>
> *She grabbed a knife from the kitchen chair and ran out to where I was hanging and got up on an old chair and cut me down. She could find no pulse; she was a nurse. When the emergency squad got to me my heart had stopped; my breath too was gone.[7]*

Michael Sabom has suggested that distressing near-death experiences with fear or bewilderment sometimes accompany the initial passage into darkness as the person ponders what is going on. As the experience progresses, these unpleasant emotions are replaced with calm, peace, or tranquility as further elements of the near-death experience begin to unfold. Bruce Greyson takes the view that the negative event may be perceived as a warning about unwise behaviors and may lead to a self-analysis and ultimately to a turnaround in one's life. Kenneth Ring has suggested that perhaps a few people get stuck in the frightening aspects of their near-death experience and are unable to move beyond it. If they could go with it, the fear might resolve into peace.

Very little research has been done that analyzes distressing near-death experiences; however, Dr. Helena Cassol, who was introduced in chapter 2, did a study of 123 near-death experiences and found 14 percent had distressing experiences.[8]

SUMMARY OF CHAPTER 5

The impact of both near-death experiences and between lives spiritual regression is profound. The near-death experience is more intense and vivid and is often a turning point and catalyst for shifting lives completely. The between lives spiritual regression process provides more understanding of the life purpose and path. Anita, for example, gained an appreciation of unity, oneness, and connection to all beings in her near-death experience. Her between lives spiritual regression, on the other hand, provided validation of her mission in this incarnation.

Despite small differences, the research comparing different stages has shown that there are strong similarities between near-death experiences and between lives spiritual regression. The consistently similar experiences in the two different processes provides stronger evidence that consciousness does survive permanent bodily death, and through reincarnation this consciousness evolves with each experience.

CONCLUSION TO PART ONE

Australian philosopher and cognitive scientist David Chalmers summed up the study of consciousness perfectly in this quote: "Consciousness poses the most baffling problems in the science of the mind. There is nothing that we know more intimately than conscious experience, but there is nothing that is harder to explain."[1]

So far, there is no universal scientific proof that consciousness exists outside the body or that consciousness exists after bodily death. But what would be required for this proof? There is compelling evidence to a rational mind that consciousness is outside the body and is perceived, filtered, and expressed through the body. In the previous chapters, we concisely presented the compelling areas of savant syndrome, lucid dreaming, telepathic communication during dreams, and terminal lucidity.

Research in the areas of mediumship and out-of-body experiences has been heavily criticized so we have not dwelt on them. If research is done in a controlled environment with noninvasive neurological scans to measure brain activity under the supervision of a neuroradiologist, then it could provide more conclusive evidence. For the time being, however, we need to rely on anecdotal accounts or have our own experience with a medium.

We have examined very compelling research around near-death experiences, which so far offers one of the most persuasive arguments that human consciousness exists outside permanent bodily death. However, we think that the best evidence to prove this is a multidisciplinary approach that includes both the near-death experience and the between lives spiritual regression research that we have presented.

What also stood out in part one was the life-changing effect these experiences had on people, especially the near-death experiences. Most had an expansion of consciousness outside of their physical bodies, bringing them a sense of inner peace, deeper intuitive insights, freedom from attachment and lack of judgment, and surrender of the ego. And the experience transformed their lives in a permanent and positive way.

This got us thinking. Do we need to experience the precipice of death to expand our consciousness? We think not. We are at a unique time in history that can help with this expansion while we are here, in our bodies, on Earth.

In part two, we look at why expanding our consciousness is important at this point in time and how it can move humanity toward a Golden Age to become part of a New Consciousness. We also provide the practical exercises our clients and students have used to expand their consciousness. However, the exercises are not magic pills for instant results. It takes courage and self-motivation to work through them, as they assist in breaking down old limitations and patterns of the Old Consciousness. This is open to all who choose to be part of it.

PART TWO

How to Create a New Consciousness for a New Earth

6
Shifting to an Awakening World

There is a river flowing now very fast. It is so great and swift that there are those who will be afraid. They will try to hold on to the shore. They will feel they are torn apart and will suffer greatly.

Know the river has its destination. The elders say we must let go of the shore, push off into the middle of the river, keep our eyes open, and our heads above water. And I say, see who is in there with you and celebrate. At this time in history, we are to take nothing personally, least of all ourselves. For the moment that we do, our spiritual growth and journey comes to a halt.

The time for the lone wolf is over. Gather yourselves! Banish the word struggle from your attitude and your vocabulary. All that we do now must be done in a sacred manner and in celebration.

We are the ones we've been waiting for.

ATTRIBUTED AS A HOPI PROPHECY

All the channeling in this book is by Reena and comes from different groups of evolved spirits of light, including the Council of Beings of Light, the Galactic Beings of Light, the Creators of Oneness, the Elders, and the Divine Mother. The following is from the Council of Beings of Light:

What the majority of beings on the planet you refer to as human do not seem to recognize is that the consciousness of Earth is stronger than them. The consciousness of Earth is quiet and most subtle, but the screaming noisy humans do not want to hear it and instead have created their own consciousness of noise that does not work cooperatively with that of Earth.

At the end of the day, if humans choose to continue to control the Earth, try to own Earth, or think that they are mightier than the Earth, and there is nothing else to minimize this, it may include eradicating them. But at this point we are thinking of minimizing the impact of humans on Earth, to raise their consciousness. So, a super-nova-like light is going to bring many things into view for all to see. It will also shake the mass consciousness of those who reside on Earth.

We have been pumping in more high vibrational energy into the planet to crack through the web of consciousness. The same will apply to people as well, and those who can manage it will increase their vibrations and live in the New Earth with increased vibrations, and those unable to manage it will leave.

Of course, this is a shedding process and needs some form of disruption to clear away for the new. These pulses will come through and will pound on the core of the fabric of consciousness around so people will feel it at a deep level. Not so much a fluttering around the head but a deep pounding right in the core of the guts. We advise you to just have plenty of rest to integrate this energy into your energy system.

It is about shattering the foundations to enable the structure to come falling down. What is important is that the planet has to shift and that all that resonate with her will shift as well. We are very happy that many people are stepping outside this illusion and looking in. And when people step outside the illusion, they feel a sense of freedom.

Periodically humanity goes through a big change. This may be related to a change of the Earth's axis pointing to different heavenly bodies, since the Earth goes through a full precession rotation, historically called the precession of the equinoxes, every 26,000 years.[1]

Dividing 26,000 by twelve, for the twelve signs of the zodiac, means that every 2,160 years, bringing in different heavenly energies and a new age. During the time of Moses around 4,000 years ago, it shifted from the age of Taurus to Aries. During the time of Jesus 2,000 years ago, it shifted from Aries to Pisces. We are now stepping into a new era from Pisces to Aquarius.

During the time of Moses, we moved from the old belief in the many gods of the Egyptians to the new belief in the one God, which eventually led to Judaism. Then the time of Jesus brought the feminine and masculine together with the divine. Jesus's teachings were very different from those of Moses, and they were able to shift people's consciousness.

We are now not only moving into a new age from Pisces to Aquarius, but we are starting a whole new precessional rotation. Perhaps that is why we are now being prepared for another shift. As the Council of Beings of Light said, Earth is being bombarded by very high vibrations that are shifting its consciousness. And because people's consciousness is part of the Earth, we need to shift to be in resonance.

Physics has proven that matter, liquids, and gases are made up of atoms vibrating at different frequencies. Quantum physics has gone further and through experiments found that photons of light are also made up of vibrating energy.[2] So it seems that everything is vibrating energy, and this can be extended to include our consciousness.

David Hawkins, in his book *Power vs. Force*,[3] allocated quantifiable vibrational energy of conscious states using kinesiology. This uses muscle testing in response to statements that have a "Yes" or "No" outcome, in which typically an extended arm is used with the arm muscles either strong or weak in response to the statements. Kinesiology is widely used for getting to the root causes of people's problems and was thought to be a local response from the body. Later research suggested it is a general response from consciousness itself. Hawkins research method built on this by tapping into the universal consciousness using muscle responses to a series of questions with each emotion and was replicated for accuracy.

He found that on a scale of 0 to 1000, negative emotions were at 150 or lower, with fear being one of the lowest vibrations at 100, and enlightenment being at the highest level of between 700 and 1000. The highest emotions associated with expanded consciousness were peace at 600, joy at 540, and love at 500.

The high vibration energy now coming into Earth will amplify the frequency of even the most minute particle. It will intensify everything around us and within us, our thoughts, our emotions, and our physical body, which holds our consciousness. So, if we carry a lot of anxiety, this will be amplified. If we carry a lot of joy, this too, will be amplified. We can see this at a global level where polarity and divisiveness are being stirred to extremes. The levels of fear, anxiety, and stress we are witnessing are high. People are more disconnected from nature and from each other. What we are witnessing is more and more breakdowns of the old systems.

The new vibrations are also breaking down long-held illusions and bringing to the surface what has been previously hidden. This is happening at both a global level and a personal level. While some of the unveilings can be shocking or disturbing, they are being brought to the forefront of our awareness so that we can see exactly what's been happening and can make our own decision about whether we want to continue to stay in the old consciousness or change and move to the new. Moving to the New Consciousness will allow for new systems that are aligned with the new vibrations of expanded consciousness to be created and upheld.

It is an individual choice and making the shift into the new is difficult. It will take a lot of courage to change. However, staying with the old will get progressively more uncomfortable. We are still newborns, and our umbilical cords are still attached to the old world. But soon they will fall off, and we will sail freely into a new cycle. The exercises in these chapters have been designed to help expand our consciousness and provide a rudder to guide us into the New Consciousness.

OUR PERSONAL EXPERIENCE OF DISCOVERING THE NEW CONSCIOUSNESS

We were in Arizona, driving down the road to Sedona with desert on both sides, when Reena looked up at the sky and became aware of what appeared to be a face in the clouds. Suddenly she heard, "We will be coming to give you a new course." She felt a bit crazy and told Andy. Three days later the Council of Beings of Light came to us in a channeling session, introduced themselves, and explained that they will be coming to give us a new course—Pioneering the New Consciousness—so we were delighted and honored. This started in 2014, and we have been transitioning into the New Consciousness as much as we can since then.

The Council of Beings of Light defined a seven-day workshop and explained what was needed to be covered in each of the days. Reena was the channel, and Andy was the scribe. We were very careful to record their words exactly as they said them and the techniques exactly as they described them. We then wrote it all into a handbook, so we could pass the information on in a very clean, pure form. This was important because at other times sacred knowledge has been twisted and distorted by the human ego, and we needed to ensure that everybody got the same information we did.

So having the framework in place, we spent a couple of years using the techniques and developing our skill and knowledge. The workshops were given in locations that supported the new vibrations: Mount Shasta in the United States, which is the Earth's energy base chakra, and Glastonbury in the UK, which is the Earth's energy heart chakra. Energetically they are very special places, and we made sure that we had a residential site so the vibration in the site as well as that of the people inside could be raised. This was to enable those in the workshop to experience and work in the energies of the New Consciousness.

WHAT WILL LIVING IN
THE NEW CONSCIOUSNESS BE LIKE?

The New Consciousness is about immersing ourselves in the new frequencies that is coming through, which will lead to understanding that all of Creation is divine and that we can live symbiotically with the Earth and with the finer energies of the Earth that we haven't been able to tap into for such a long time.

It is quite hard to say what everybody's life is going to be like in the New Consciousness because we are still thinking from the perspective of the old one. It's almost like a baby that has to be born first before it starts to grow and develop. We've been conditioned by the old consciousness through our education, what our friends say, the jobs we have had, and what the media says. Part of the shift is letting go of all of this, which is really hard to do—rather like giving birth. It can be a little painful but once the birth is finished, we can start to grow and flourish.

Perhaps a few examples from our workshops will help to give you an idea of how things can be different.

One student from a different country was single when she came to the workshop. Because she was in the high vibration of the workshop, everything within her shifted. Afterward she went off on a weekend retreat, fell in love with a soul mate, got married, and now has a family. She credits the shift of her energies from the New Consciousness for this big change in her life.

In the workshops we embrace New Consciousness energies. Some students use energies for healing diseases or illness energetically, since they are all fundamentally energy problems. If you raise the vibration of the area affected in the right way, it speeds up the body's ability to heal naturally.

A dramatic example of this was during one of the workshops with a student who had a prostate problem. For a number of years whenever he went to the toilet he had incredible pain passing water. There was a point in the workshop when students worked in pairs using the New Consciousness energies to resolve a physical problem. He asked his colleague to work on his prostate and half an hour later he went to the toilet and was pain-free. The session took two to three minutes and was a remarkable demonstration of how powerful these energies are.

Another example of using the New Consciousness energies is a student who is an artist and is now channeling these energies into paintings so that when the purchaser looks at the picture, they feel and absorb the energy. Authors have put the energy into the words of the books as they write to reach people that way. A singer can use singing as a way of passing the high vibrations through the songs.

When we absorb and immerse ourselves in the New Consciousness energies, we shift our own vibrations to embrace the New Earth and break away from the illusions of the old consciousness. Everything that is in resonance with the new frequencies that we hold will be attracted to us. And everything in dissonance will drop away. Take the way we consume things, for example. Maybe we do not need the latest fashion or gadget as much as we think we do and can continue to use what we already have instead of throwing perfectly good items into a landfill.

EFFECT ON RELATIONSHIPS

A soul moving to the New Consciousness will find it increasingly challenging to live with a partner, family relation, or business colleague who is still in the old consciousness. It will not feel right vibrationally. It is a soul choice to stay either in the old consciousness or wake up and move on to New Consciousness. It is not about trying to fix the issue but about respecting the free will of the other soul and letting go. New relationships with those in a similar vibration will happen quickly, and it will feel right being with them.

NEW CONSCIOUSNESS JOURNAL

A program with exercises to start expanding consciousness starts in this chapter and runs through to the end of the book. This has been designed to help with the journey to the New Consciousness. Keeping a journal for this program will be helpful, so perhaps you can buy a small notebook with a cover that you feel drawn to. In this you can write the exercises, a summary of what you do, and the positive changes that come about in your life. Enjoy yourself, have an open mind, and work with love.

NEW CONSCIOUSNESS LIFESTYLE CHANGES

Our physical body needs to be fit to handle the higher vibrational energy of the New Consciousness. It is the temple within which our soul resides and needs looking after in terms of getting regular exercise, eating healthy foods, and avoiding excess drugs and alcohol.

The cycle of life has been created to provide food for all living creatures, and we are free to choose which part of this cycle we eat from, whether it is only vegetables or includes fish and animal meat. What is important is that we have the right balance of nutrients and that whatever food is eaten has been looked after with love and, if possible, grown in a high-vibration setting. The love or high vibrational energy will be absorbed in the food and then passed to us when it is eaten.

Ultraprocessed foods have grown rampant in popularity because of their convenience. These include soft drinks, sweet or savory packaged snacks, reconstituted meat products, and pre-prepared frozen dishes. They are not natural foods but formulations from substances derived from food and with additives and little intact natural food or nutrients. Additives in ultraprocessed foods include preservatives, antioxidants, and stabilizers.

As our vibrations shift, we will find that we are drawn to different sorts of food that has a vibration similar to our natural physical bodies and with the nutrients we need. Our bodies act as our communication tool. For example, some of our clients have found that foods with a lot of refined sugar do not agree with their body, and they get symptoms of physical discomfort, like headaches. Also, prolonged consumption of food with the wrong vibrations has led to eczema, allergic reactions, a foggy mind, and gut problems. However, when they move to food that has a vibration similar to their body, their mind is clearer, they have more energy, their stomach feels right, and their allergies resolve. These are organic changes that can be expected over a number of years. When we follow the vibration of our bodies, we become physically healthier and better able to hold the higher vibrations.

Ideally drinking two quarts of water a day is optimal.[4] This helps to flush out toxins from the body that have built up from the food eaten, and it makes it easier for the high vibrational energies of the New Consciousness to be conducted by the body.

We also need to take care of our emotional body. As mentioned earlier, David Hawkins discovered that the energy of negative emotions, especially fear, carried the lowest vibrations, and those associated with an expanded consciousness had the highest. So, to hold the higher vibrations we need to clear negative emotions, and there is a self-help exercise called Tapping Away Emotions later in the chapter that can help.

Stress also affects the body's ability to hold the higher frequencies. In his book *The Biology of Belief*, Bruce Lipton, a renowned cell biologist, explained that humans are multicellular organisms with two separate protection systems for the maintenance of life.[5] The first is protection against external threats, which happens when the body creates adrenaline to prepare the body for flight or fight. This is normally based on the emotion of fear, which in the modern world is often caused by a perceived threat rather than a real one. The second is the immune system that protects the body from bacteria and viruses and when fully operating can consume much of the body's energy supply. If the adrenal system is triggered, it shuts down the immune system to focus the body's energy on the immediate threat.

Prolonged stress—called chronic stress—has a major effect on the immune system, and Sebastian Brandhorst, a specialist in cell and molecular biology, found in his research that almost every major illness that people acquire is linked to chronic stress.[6]

Stress comes from a perceived threat or underestimating our ability to handle a situation in our environment and often has the underlying emotion of fear attached. So, fear not only lowers our body's vibrational energy, it creates stress and lowers the immune system, making us more susceptible to illness. In the old consciousness the levels of fear, anxiety, and stress we experience have been high, and the stronger vibrations coming to Earth intensify these emotions that are held in our bodies. The more anxiety and fear, the more discomfort we feel.

We can either stay in the lifestyle of the old consciousness or change our lifestyle to prepare our bodies and expand our consciousness to move to the New Consciousness. The more that peace, love, and joy can be amplified, the more comfortable we will become.

✧ Exercise: Making Lifestyle Changes

Lifestyle changes include eating the right food, reducing stress and fear, and improving the environment we live in.

1. Start a section in your journal for food. Choose foods using the wisdom of your body and after a meal, write down what you ate and then write down your answers to the following questions: How does your stomach feel? How is your energy level? Are you experiencing physical discomfort like a foggy mind or allergies? There are many fine books about natural food that can inspire you to change your food until it's right for your body.

2. Add a section in your journal for the stress, anxiety, and fear in your life. Identify the areas that cause these emotions, and as you progress through this book, use the exercises to help you reduce them. Possible stressful areas to think about are your work, family, relationships, and general lifestyle. Give them a priority. Decide which area(s) you want to start with first and the date you will begin to make any necessary

changes. Make a commitment to yourself. Record the changes you will make in your journal and plan other changes in a similar way.

OLD EMOTIONAL WOUNDS

Old emotional issues, when triggered, hold us in a lower vibration, so they need to be cleared. Some of these may have their roots in childhood issues, which are often associated with the loss of love. Although the original memory may be below the level of conscious awareness, it affects us in later life with repetitive patterns of emotions and behaviors that were the child's coping ways at the time the issue was created. See which coping behaviors or emotions you identify with in the following examples.

The Pleaser

When Joan was young her father was a self-employed dock worker and only got paid for the day he was offered work. Often, he would go for weeks without work, and when he did work, it was hard manual labor, and the stress of it caused him to drink heavily. He would arrive home drunk and looking for someone to take out his frustrations on, so little Joan quickly learned to be quiet and do whatever she could to be a "good girl." She would read a situation and anticipate what would happen to avoid trouble.

Joan ended up marrying an emotionally abusive husband and was given very little money for housekeeping or support to bring up the family, so her pleasing pattern continued. After she left her husband, she did everything she could to please her now adult daughters and would spend weeks making special meals for family gatherings. If her efforts were not appreciated, she would burst into tears, as being appreciated was her way of getting love.

Joan's coping behavior involved suppressing her feelings and desires so that everyone would like her. Later in life, it became a habit of not valuing herself, doing anything for a quiet life, and often feeling guilty. The thought from her subconscious memory was I can only relax when everyone has everything they want.

The Achiever

Javad was a highflier in industry. He graduated with a first-class degree and was headhunted by a major computer company. He completed a research project quicker than expected and was given an outstanding new employee of the year award. He went on to manage two hundred of the world's top scientists in a multimedia research lab. He was then headhunted by a $200 million turnover computer company to be their CEO. He often only slept for four hours a night because there was so much to do.

Javad's father had been a surgeon in Iran who had worked his way up from poverty and wanted to instill the same work ethic in his children. He regularly interrogated Javad on how he was doing at school in front of the family, and Javad was left feeling humiliated and unloved. Javad's inner child was still trying to get love from his father by achieving success in business, but nothing was ever enough.

Javad's coping behavior was trying harder and harder to prove to the memory of his parents that he was good enough to be loved and always hearing a voice in his head saying, *You could have done better.* Later in life, he became an overstressed workaholic.

The Rebel

When Brian was a young child his father worked late-night shifts, and the household had to be quiet during the day when he slept. His father never adjusted to shift work. He was always tired and irritable, and he never had time for little Brian. There was one traumatic time when his father locked Brian under the stairs in the dark and left him there as a punishment. Brian screamed the house down, and his father, realizing the effect of his action, released him. For Brian, this started a pattern of acting rebellious when he was confronted with someone trying to control him.

Brian's coping behavior as a child was to do something naughty and make a fuss. Although this meant trouble for him, it at least got him attention. Later in life, his behavior was to shock people and get angry to get his own way or needed attention.

The Victim

Linda was the youngest of a family of five, and her single-parent mother coped as well as she could, holding down two jobs to bring in money for them all to survive. Being the youngest and often with no adult supervision, Linda was constantly picked on by the other children. Also, her mother always seemed to blame Linda for the problems in her life. But Linda found that when she cried, she got helpful attention. When she got married, the pattern continued, and her husband found it easier to do everything for her rather than have her in tears. This perpetuated her victim role.

Linda's coping behavior as a child was to cry enough to get some love and attention. Later in life, when things went wrong, it was always someone else's fault. She never took responsibility for her life because if she did, no one would look after her.

The Rationalizer

When Anne was three, her mother screamed and shouted at her father as he stormed out of the house for the final time. Then her mother shouted abuse at Anne, saying it was all Anne's fault that her father had left, that she was useless, and that she wished Anne had never been born. At school, other children took great delight in teasing and bullying her, tripping her up and saying cruel and nasty things to her. Her teacher also treated her coldly by picking on her in class and humiliating her in front of the rest of the children. These were the times she learned that emotions were dangerous, and it was safer to avoid them and stay in her head.

Anne's coping behavior was to live in her head because it was the safest place to be. Emotions expressed in her family scared her because they were overwhelming. It was safer to disconnect from her feelings, so as a child she never cried or got angry, and she never learned how to deal with her feelings. Later in life she could not remember the last time she had been angry or sad.

The Rescuer

John's father was a no-good alcoholic, so John took his father's place by becoming extremely close to his mother and protecting her. He later married a cold, emotionless wife and started to have a series of affairs with needy women. Every time he had an affair, the woman became a mother image in his mind, and he wanted to protect her and receive her love in return. Despite promising his wife not to cheat again, the pattern continued.

John's coping behavior was to be attracted to victims so he could look after them and help them with their problems, which meant he did not have to pay attention to his own. And rescuing women kept them dependent on him, and left him in control and needed.

RESOLVING OLD EMOTIONAL PATTERNS

One windy day in 1987, psychologist Francine Shapiro, a senior research fellow at the Mental Research Institute in Palo Alto, California, was out walking. While watching leaves falling nearby, she was thinking about some disturbing issues. Finishing her walk, she was amazed to discover that her troubling thoughts had disappeared and that they seemed to have lost their emotional charge. Assuming that this was a result of the eye movements she had unwittingly performed during her walk, Francine proceeded to experiment on volunteers to see if she could reproduce the effect. Achieving positive results, she then proceeded to develop the technique, and it was successfully tested on people suffering from emotional trauma issues. The traumatized volunteers were instructed to move their eyes rapidly from side to side while visualizing disturbing scenes, which resulted in the memories becoming less and less disturbing.[7]

Eventually it was discovered that other ways work equally well, like alternately tapping on different areas of the body or alternating sounds between the left and right ears. This showed that the effectiveness of the procedure was not simply a result of the rapid eye movement we all experience when asleep as was first thought.

When a person with an emotional memory is encouraged to focus on that memory as fully as possible using all of their senses while alternate bilateral stimulation is applied, their natural information processing system is activated. This is a mind-body free-associative process that activates both left and right hemispheres of the brain, affecting the physical storage of the emotional memory so that it no longer feels disturbing. Dr. Shapiro found she had to do several sessions with each subject, monitored by a trained therapist.

Fred Friedberg, an associate professor in the Applied Behavioral Medicine Research Institute in New York, produced a shortened self-help form for people to safely use on emotional issues at home. This is relatively simple and involves alternate tapping with the fingers, left-right, at a rate of around two taps per second and continuing for a round lasting approximately three minutes at a time. One tap on the left quickly followed by one tap on the right, repeated for the duration of the round. He found that if there was no improvement after three rounds of tapping then rounds of eye movements could be introduced.[8]

✧ Exercise: Tapping Away Emotions

1. If the emotion that causes you stress is not present right now, it needs to be re-created. Close your eyes and focus on the memory of the last time or worst time the emotion occurred and let an image, feeling, or thought surface. If necessary, think of the worst part of that memory using all of your senses and give yourself permission for the emotion to arise. If a physical sensation such as headache, clenched jaw, stomach discomfort, or any general physical tension starts as well, let it happen. Rate the emotion you experience on a scale of 0 to 10, with 0 being no discomfort at all, and 10 being the worst it could be.

2. With the symptoms still present start tapping alternately on your thighs, so your right finger(s) taps your right thigh, then your left thigh, then the right again and so on, two taps per second for three minutes. Whether you use one finger or more to tap is unimportant.

3. Take a deep breath and reassess the stress level.

4. If it is decreasing in severity, continue with further rounds of tapping until 1 or 0 is reached. If any new stresses emerge, then it may be necessary to continue tapping to remove them.

5. If there is no decrease in severity, perform twenty-five to thirty rapid eye movements from side to side. Keep the head still and choose a suitable object in your extreme left field of vision and one in your extreme right to focus on and then alternate looking from one to the other.

6. If there is improvement after two rounds of rapid eye movements, continue until 1 or 0 is reached.

7. If there is still no improvement, it could indicate a deep trauma that requires the help of a therapist professionally trained to resolve deeper emotional wounds such as those in the Spiritual Regression Therapy Association[9] or Earth Association for Regression Therapy.[10]

HEALING RELATIONSHIP ISSUES

If you are experiencing relationship issues, you can try an ancient Hawaiian healing process called ho'oponopono to heal them. The basic principle of ho'oponopono states that we need to take total responsibility for our lives and that we should not blame others for anything. This means that anything going on in the world—terrorist activity, government actions, the economy, and so on—or anything we experience in our personal lives or relationships that brings up negative emotions is something we, ourselves, need to heal. The problem isn't with "them," it's with us, and we have to change ourselves to change the relationship or situation.

So if you have a persistent unhelpful thought or emotion about a situation or another person, one way to take responsibility for it is to repetitively say the ho'oponopono mantra, "I love you, I'm sorry, please forgive me, thank you" until your emotion or thought changes.

And because energy follows thought, you can combine this mantra with the intention of sending love energy to the other person. This involves creating an energy link from your heart to the heart of the other person and then using the mantra of "I love you, I forgive you, I love myself, I forgive myself" and repeating it until your emotion or troublesome thought changes.

✧ Exercise: Using the Ho'oponopono Mantra

The next time you have a conflict with a partner, friend, or family member and are perhaps feeling angry at how you have been treated or regret something you said, find a quiet place away from others, create an energy link from your heart to theirs with the intent to send love, and repeat either of the mantras suggested above. You will be amazed at the change in yourself and how it also shifts the emotional state of the person it is directed at—but give it time to have an effect.

CLEARING BLOCKED ENERGY

The use of different-colored lights has been used since the ancient civilizations of Egypt, Greece, China, and India to treat mental distress and physical symptoms. Colors are simply different vibrations of natural light and can be used to benefit the body and the aura around it in other ways. In color therapy these different vibrations can be used to clear blocked energy from emotions and unwanted thoughts in our aura. It lets the blocked energy flow and then the emotional energy and unwanted thoughts can be released.

✧ Exercise: Applying Color Therapy

Before trying this exercise, read through the steps a few times first. Then when you have memorized them, go through the process with your eyes closed so you are not distracted by having to read the next step. You may be able to do this by yourself, but we suggest initially getting help from your spirit guide by just asking them quietly or aloud. You will find inspiration will come to you from your guide, so there is no need to analytically work things out.

1. If the unwanted thought or emotion is not present it needs to be re-created by focusing on it. Give it a rating on a scale of 0 and 10, with 0 being no discomfort at all and 10 being the worst it could be.
2. Identify the location in your body where the unwanted thought or emotion resides and point to it to make it clearer to you. If there is more than one location, work with the strongest first and then later repeat the exercise for the others.
3. Weaken the hold that the energy of the thought or emotion has on you by creating an "object" to represent it. Imagine its texture, color, and shape. An example could be a smooth black sphere.
4. Ask yourself what color is needed to weaken the object (smooth black

sphere). We are using the imagination so there is no right or wrong. Ask for whatever color pops into your mind to come down, swirl it around the object, and decide how the object's texture, color, and shape changes. You may see it or feel it or just know it—whichever way it comes to you is fine. An example could be a blue light swirling around the smooth black sphere and changing it to a fluffy white cloud.

The color that comes to you will bring its own vibrational energy to help in the transformation. The exercise can be repeated with other colors if you wish.

5. Decide on the best way to discharge the energy. Perhaps you can pull it out with your hands or blow it out of your mouth; do whatever you feel is best physically to discharge the energy. You can ask it to go to Mother Earth or a psychic dustbin, or you can ask your spirit guide to take it away so that the energy is not lying around your room.

6. After clearing the unwanted energy, it is useful to bring in positive energy by bringing a new color in where the old one was. Imagine the object having this new color along with a new shape and notice what quality it brings with it. An example could be a yellow shining sun bringing in peace.

7. What thought(s) and emotion(s) come with this new object? Check in to see what the level of the old emotion or thought is. The level should be a 0 or 1 on the scale. If not, repeat the process.

REACHING FORGIVENESS

Katja Rosenberg was cycling home after work when she was attacked by a sixteen-year-old stranger. She was punched in the face, chest, and stomach before being raped. He was jailed for fourteen years after admitting to the attack and also the rape of a fifty-one-year-old woman shortly afterward.

Later Katja said, "Life deals very different cards to all of us, and while somebody who does this is not applaudable, it is more about thinking something is wrong with society. Some of us don't know where to go. You wouldn't ever do this if you felt happy."[11] She always felt she would eventually meet her attacker and finally visited him in prison for a meeting arranged through the restorative justice scheme with the support of the Probation Service.

This was partially motivated by her wish to assure him, "Life is not hopeless, so he knows he has got a future." What was important for her was to walk in the same direction of peace and forgiveness together.

She found that forgiveness and closure is a key to untold peace and happiness. It is not easy, especially when a person has done something we find unforgivable and there is a strong emotional charge associated. However, with forgiveness we become free of the emotional weights of resentment, anger, self-doubt, and guilt that have been hurting us. And we allow our heart and mind to guide us.

Everyone has their own unique path to forgiveness. If it is not reached in this life there will be opportunities in a future life, but it lowers our vibration in this life and stops us moving to the New Consciousness. It is not right or wrong, just a soul choice with different consequences.

True forgiveness enables the letting go of painful, pent-up emotions and negative core beliefs. These emotions are a message from the universe to bring it to our attention that an issue needs to be addressed.

All humans have inherent imperfections. Many perpetrators had similar things happen to them when they were young. This awareness is more likely to occur after spending time reflecting on the events and circumstances and communicating with the other person.

It is helpful to accept that the event has happened and that we are responsible for our own emotions. For example, if someone has a phobia of spiders, they can blame the spider, but the spider is not responsible for creating the emotion of fear. Forgiveness often involves understanding the background and intent of the other person directly or intuitively to be able to let go of unhelpful thoughts toward them that hold the emotion in place.

✧ Exercise: Imagining a Path to Forgiveness

1. It may be necessary to experience and release painful emotions before finding forgiveness. Katja was able to release her emotions by meeting the man who raped her. When forgiveness is needed, try meeting and speaking to the other person from a place of compassion and honesty. Ask them about their intention of the event that caused the pain and their perspective of the events.

2. If this is not possible, with your eyes closed, imagine they are in front of you and say what you could not say at the time about your pain. Imagine what they might say back to you about what happened.

3. Imagine a box of any size and place all your pain and hurt into the box. Then imagine passing the box to the other person. You can choose to have the box lid open, so the other person feels all your hurt and pain, or you can close the lid and surround the box with love and pass it to them.

4. Ask to let go of any soul energy from the other person that you are holding and reclaim any of your soul energy back from that person.

5. Reflect on what these events have taught you and in what way you have spiritually grown as a soul. Write all your findings in your journal.

SUMMARY OF CHAPTER 6

The arrival of the New Consciousness is like the tide. Whether we believe in it or not makes no difference because it is commanded by forces beyond our control. All we can do if we are on the beach and the tide is coming in is to take action by moving farther up the beach. If we don't, the situation just gets worse, and we are bound to get wet.

This chapter started you on your journey to the New Consciousness.

We suggested that you create a journal to record your journey through the exercises here and those to come later on. The first step is to make lifestyle changes to prepare your physical body to hold the higher vibrations of the New Consciousness. The second step is to take responsibility for your emotions and not to blame others. The self-help techniques in this chapter can help you to reduce your emotional symptoms. Symptoms that do not fully respond could indicate deeper issues, and there are many professionally trained therapists that can help. The last step is the power of forgiveness. This comes after releasing the associated emotions and finding out the background and intent of the person who hurt you.

It is strong to forgive, but it is stronger to let go and find freedom.

7
Energy Management

Leave the familiar for a while.
Let your senses and bodies stretch out.

HAFIZ, FOURTEENTH-CENTURY PERSIAN
MYSTIC AND POET

———————— ✧ ————————

It was only when my beautiful daughter was born that I suddenly became aware of other people's energy. I received information through my inner voice not just about me but about others. I started feeling presences around me and I could also read their energy when I directed my awareness toward them. I started having trouble sleeping at night since these presences would wake me up as if saying, "Hello, I'm here."

I decided to search for answers to better understand what was happening. At one point I felt an emotional vibration enter the room and my body. I had no control over the situation. The emotion took over my body and I was in great sadness and I could not stop the feeling.

My therapist took me outside where I was able to release the excess energy and ground myself. Later that day I was taught how

I could block these vibrations from entering my body by creating an
intentional protection to shield me, like a cloak. These structures
enabled me to be in control of the energies . . . and to feel more
empowered.

The preceding account detailed an emerging spiritual emergency of
Reena's client who we will call Melanie. This can happen when intangible energies overwhelm a person's physical, mental, and emotional
consciousness.[1]

In Melanie's case it was caused by the birth of her daughter, but
it could have been caused by an accident, unsupervised spiritual practice, extreme stress, or the use of psychoactive mind-expanding drugs.
While most people do not normally experience the extremes of a spiritual emergency, many of us can experience some early stages, or we can
feel overwhelmed by day-to-day events.

When our bodily consciousness is overwhelmed, it is very difficult
to tap into the subtle intangible soul. Imagine a radio with the volume
turned up too high—it blasts and blinds our other senses. The skill is
to know how to turn down the volume so it does not overpower the
connection with our soul. This chapter will cover tips for doing this by
managing and grounding our physical body.

MINDFULNESS

Mindfulness is an important part of managing any stage of a spiritual emergency or a feeling of being overwhelmed. Its simplicity and
effectiveness for coping with many conditions has enabled it to cross
into mainstream Western medicine, and it is now used within the
UK and the US health care systems. Mindfulness can be incredibly effective in many situations, and it is reputed to be particularly
helpful during dissociation, panic attacks, strong impulsive urges,

flashbacks, severe anxiety, and intense emotional distress.[2]

To practice mindfulness means to focus on the present by using our five physical senses to experience everything in the moment we are in, however mundane and inconsequential, and to avoid thinking about the future or past. For example, if you're carrying out a routine chore such as washing the car, you focus purely on the task at hand. On the temperature of the soapy water, the sensations you experience as you move the wet sponge over the car, the feeling of your feet touching the ground beneath you, the actions of your body as you move and stretch, the sounds around you, the smell of the cleaning agent, even the brightness of the paint as you shine the car. When your awareness is solely in the present moment and all thoughts are focused on the details your senses are taking in, you naturally become embodied, putting unhelpful thoughts out of the mind.

✧ Exercise: Practicing Mindfulness

The next time you feel overwhelmed or just have a worrying thought, do a mindfulness exercise. Start with ten minutes and go longer if necessary. Consider a physical activity like walking in nature, working in the garden, or cleaning the house. While the concept is simple, to keep yourself in the Now and out of your head, it does take practice and determination, but just like building a muscle it becomes easier over time.

GROUNDING

A student we will call Charlie joined our regression therapy training. She had been doing shamanic journeying for many years previously and after the first day of the workshop at Mount Shasta in California went down to a sacred place and did her shamanic ritual. What she had failed to realize was that the energy around Mount Shasta is very strong, and care is needed when doing out-of-body experiences there.

When she arrived back at the residential accommodation she was in a sorry state, unfocused and totally out of her body. Recognizing the symptoms, Reena immediately started grounding activities. As it was a warm summer night, Charlie was asked to take off her shoes and feel the cool grass on her feet, allowing her to discharge excess energy to the ground. Then she was encouraged to stamp her feet to bring her focus into her body. As she started to become grounded Reena gave her a drink and at that point was able to find out what had happened.

Grounding helps bring our conscious focus back to the body. It is like the roots of a tree needing to be in the Earth to stay stable and grow. When people have been in an out-of-body experience, trance, or deep meditation, their consciousness needs to be grounded.

✧ Exercise: Performing Grounding Techniques

Easy techniques for grounding include spending time in nature, moving the body, breathing deeply, drinking, eating, or stamping the feet. Another method is called Cook's Hookup. In addition to grounding, this integrates the left and right sides of the brain and reduces confusion and lack of coordination. It is best to perform this exercise while sitting in a chair.

1. Cross your ankles, right over left.
2. Cross your wrists in front of you, right over left.
3. Now twist your hands so the palms are facing each other and interlace your fingers.
4. Roll your hands down and up through the circle of your arms and toward your chest, letting your elbows move downward.
5. Relax, close your eyes, and breathe easily.
6. When you feel calm and restored to normal balance, unclasp your hands and uncross your ankles. Place your feet flat on the floor.

KEEPING OUR ENERGY CLEAR

Just as it is important to keep our home and personal body physically clean on a regular basis, it is also important to periodically clear the energetic body. This will help restore a calm, still state from which we can access our eternal soul.

An easy technique to clear our energy is to take a shower or bath and set an intention that any energies not belonging to us will be washed away. Alternatively, visualize yourself standing in a waterfall of pure clearing energy that flows over your whole body and through all the organs and chakra points. Set the intent for any energies not belonging to you to flow with the cleaning energy into the Earth.

To clear a room energetically, sweep a selenite crystal around the space with the intention of brushing away any energetic debris. The room can also be smudged with sage, sweet grass, cedar, sandalwood, incense, or other clearing smoke. One end of the smudge stick is set alight so that it smolders and produces a fragrant, cleansing smoke. This smoke is then fanned around the room. Toning, bell ringing, drumming, chanting, and other forms of sound clearing as well as essential oils, mists, and flower essences are also effective. Whatever technique and medium are used, set the intention to clear any energies not belonging to the room.

Every time we take a low vibration out it is useful to put a high vibration back in. Perhaps ask for the love energy from Source or the Oneness to come and fill yourself or the room.

ENERGY PROTECTION

When I first became a therapist some of my colleagues practicing Reiki energy healing mentioned that they used energy protection to avoid becoming drained of energy at the end of a day of work. I found this interesting, but I never had any problems with being drained of energy so I put it to one side. Over the years, as I cleared more of my emotional issues my intuition and energy sensitivity increased.

While in Spain a contact arranged to see me for a few hours about a new initiative. Eventually I spent the whole day in discussion with her and having a leisurely meal. She seemed very negative about many things. In the afternoon I started to feel tired but just put it down to too much concentration. When I got home at the end of the day, I collapsed on my bed totally drained of energy and had to take the next day off work to slowly recover. I had been a victim of an energy vampire and for the whole of the meeting energy had been drained from me. It hadn't been intentional on her part, but it happened anyway.

This was a personal experience that happened to Andy, but it is all too familiar and could apply to anyone. As the mental and emotional bodies become clearer, and we access and work from our soul, our vibration rises. Our energy changes from being a dim light to being a lighthouse in the darkness of the world. It then becomes so much more important to protect ourselves from being drained or attracting unwanted energies.

Whenever we are around other people, we are exposing ourselves to their subtle energies. Most of the time these energies are positive. However, there are times when people have lower vibrational energies caused by negative thoughts and emotions, and these can drain our energy. Perhaps you can recall a time when you were talking to someone feeling depressed and after a while you felt drained of energy, or you were in a crowded train or plane for a period of time and were glad to just be back in your own private space.

Our energy field is called an aura and normally acts as a protective screen to block out and repel the negative energies of others and also prevents leakage of our own energy. However, a tear or weakness in our aura can make it possible for other energies to enter. This can be caused by stress, trauma, depression, drugs, abuse, physical injuries, or illnesses. Protection is about strengthening our energy aura. The clearer our aura, the less likely we are to get caught up in the whirlwind of external negativity, and the easier it will be to go within and work from our soul consciousness.

One technique is to ask for an energy bubble to be placed around us and set the intention, "Only energy for my highest good can enter my bubble and any unneeded energy can exit." We can set the intention for the bubble energy to come from Source or Mother Earth or both for extra protection. Visualization can be used but the intention still has to be made. It is useful to reinforce this on a regular basis such as whenever we meditate.

Another technique is to use crystals such as black shungite, onyx, or smoky quartz. They can be worn or carried in a pocket.

Protection can be put around a room or a house by asking for Source energy to create a bubble around the house or workplace to allow energies for the highest good to come through and any energies no longer needed to move on.

Also, protection is needed from items in the house that radiate electromagnetic energy. A small shungite disc can be attached to mobile phones to reduce the radiation from them, and a shungite crystal can be placed next to internet routers. Microwave ovens and induction cookers are best replaced with alternative technology items. Some people switch the internet off at night with a time switch to minimize radiation while they sleep.

OPENING AND CLOSING THE CHAKRAS

We all have seven energy centers called chakras that help the flow of energy around the body and managing them can also provide energy protection. Our chakras open and close quite naturally. If we go into nature and feel wonderful, our energy field naturally opens to embrace the experience. If we cross our arms in an uncomfortable situation, it is like saying, Nothing can come in.

When we are with friends or meditating, it is useful to open our chakras to fully connect with our intuition. When we are in a crowd of people such as on public transportation or are spending time with negative people, it is much better to close our chakras to minimize taking in any negative energy.

Each chakra can be opened by imagining it like a flower and, by intention, allowing the petals to open. When they are all open imagine your energy aura like a bubble that expands into the distance and set the intention to be able to energetically connect with the universe. Each chakra can be closed by imagining the petals in the flower closing.

A simpler way is to set the intention for all your chakras to fully open or all of them to fully close at once. What is important is not having your chakras permanently closed for long periods, as it stops the natural flow of energy around the body and can eventually lead to ill health.

✧ Exercise: Protecting Your Energy

Write down and explore the following in your journal.

1. List the reasons why you think energy protection is needed.
2. Which method of energy protection will you use to protect your personal energy field when you're in large groups of people or traveling in congested situations?
3. How will you energetically clear your home and workspace and how frequently will you do it?

ENERGY CORD CUTTING

Emotional interactions or traumatic situations between people can lead to soul fragments splitting off from one person and attaching to the other. It can happen in situations of severe or prolonged loss, pain, trauma, fear, or grief. We don't always know consciously that we have lost something as it happens automatically.

A client I will call Veronica said she felt like some things in her life were blocked and seemed so hard to do. This is what she wrote:

> I connected to my problem. It seems like in the past I had some sort of agreement with someone not to expand or share my Light. The spiritual workshops I attended over a weekend in Switzerland brought this more to my attention. Intuitively I made the intent to talk to the person even though I was not conscious who it was. I asked for the energetic bonds to be cleared and any soul energy of theirs that I was holding to be returned. And any energy of mine to come back to me, clean and cleared. I instantly felt better.

✧ Exercise: Cutting the Energy Cord

1. Try to recall an event you experienced with a person who is affecting you. If one does not spring to mind, set the intention before you go to sleep that you will remember one when you wake up.
2. Intentionally ask for the energy cord to the other person to be cut and any soul energy you have been holding from them to be released.
3. Then ask that your soul energy be returned from the other person.
4. Notice how you feel now and repeat for other situations or people.

SPIRIT ATTACHMENTS

As a student I had arranged to do a past life session with an elderly lady born in the Caribbean who spoke very softly. Entering a past life became difficult and suddenly she said in a loud gruff male voice, "What do you want?" I was completely taken aback by what was happening, so I decided to bring her out of hypnosis trance to talk to her. She started to talk in her normal quiet voice again, so I asked her if she could explain the loud gruff voice. She said, "Oh, that's my father. He died two years ago. My mum is in there with him but you never got around to talking to her."

This is an account Andy had when he was still a student. A spirit attachment is the discarnate spirit of someone who has died and not transcended for some reason and has instead become attached to a person.

Psychiatrist Alan Sanderson first detected and released spirit attachments in St. Thomas's Hospital in London in 1991. After his retirement he began lecturing on the practice of spirit release at the Royal College of Psychiatrists in London.[3]

It seems that after death sometimes a soul consciousness does not immediately return to the spirit realms, and they remain earthbound for a variety of reasons: they are not aware they are dead, they want to stay close to a loved one on the earth plane, they have a fear of what may happen when they go to the light, or they are too strongly attracted to the material world. Sometimes it is because the unsolved negative energy they are holding makes it difficult to respond to the pull home.

Spirits can either be lightly attached at the edges of a person's energy field or deep inside them on an emotional hook. The hook is from an emotional crisis earlier in life that provided an opening in the energy field for the discarnate spirit to enter. It is like a form of psychic resonance between the unsolved emotions of the discarnate spirit and the person's current life emotional issue. This is important to know because after the attached spirit is removed, the person's current life issues need to be resolved to remove the hook. Otherwise, it becomes an opening for other discarnate energies to attach to in the future.

Symptoms of Spirit Attachments

Fringe spirit attachments, where the energy sits at the very outside of a person's energy system, may just cause a few symptoms such as a headache or feeling low in energy.

When spirit attachments are much deeper, their unresolved emotions affect the person too. There can be a merging of thought processes so that unwanted or unusual thoughts and emotional outbursts may come from the spirit attachment. A person may feel drawn toward some behavior they would not normally do.[4] If a person has a weak ego, perhaps from a mental health issue or excessive use of drugs that overload the body, the spirit attachment may appear to live through the host and even to take them over in some way. These are called obsessive spirit attachments.

✧ Exercise: Detecting and Clearing Spirit Attachments

When we write with our nondominant hand we have to focus on the unfamiliar manner in which we are writing, and this stops thoughts about anything else and makes the use of intuition easier.

1. To test the process, sit comfortably in a quiet setting and ask your spirit guide a question on any topic.
2. On a piece of paper, begin to write freely with your nondominant hand anything that comes to you. Do not lift the pen from the paper and be sure to write in cursive. At first you will be writing slowly and

perhaps agonizing over the formation of letters. Be patient, even if your writing resembles abstract art more than language.

3. As you begin to find the process easier, ask your spirit guide how many spirit attachments you have. Then ask them to clear these attachments from you and to let you know when they have been cleared. You may also begin to feel lighter, which is another indication that the attachments are gone.

4. Alternatively, you can confirm the presence and removal of spirit attachments through your intuition or by using a pendulum.

Many spirit attachments that are on the edge of the energy field can be removed quickly by your spirit guide. For spirits attached deep in your energy field, you may need the specialized skills of a trained therapist, such as those belonging to the Spiritual Regression Therapy Association[5] or the Earth Association of Regression Therapy.[6]

Avoiding Spirit Attachments in the Future

When it rains, we put on a raincoat for protection. This does not mean we do not get wet, but it does minimize the degree of drenching we experience. Likewise, we need to use energy protection and be vigilant in places where we are at higher risk from spirit attachments. This could be in crowded spaces where we are packed close to other people, such as traveling in a plane or train. It could be in a hospital, particularly as a patient, because our energy field may be weakened by medication or an operation and make us susceptible to spirits whose bodies have recently died in the hospital. Also, at parties or any places where excessive alcohol or drugs may be consumed. If you cannot avoid these situations, before entering, close your chakras, draw your energy field close to the body by intention, and request stronger energy for your energy protection bubble.

SUMMARY OF CHAPTER 7

Energy management is important and consists of protecting and cleaning the energy in ourselves, our workplace, and our home on a regular basis. If our energy is not managed properly, any evolution to the higher vibration of the New Consciousness will be held back.

8

Boundaries for
the New
Consciousness

*The only people who get upset at you creating boundaries
are the ones benefiting from you having none.*

AUTHOR UNKNOWN

———————— ✧ ————————

*John came for therapy and said he only had half an hour available
because he had not told his wife he was coming for therapy. He asked
if he could do some artwork for me instead of paying with money
because every time he needed some money he had to ask his wife for
it. She managed all their joint money and often did not approve his
requests.*

*What surprised me much more was when he told me his life
story. He had started his own companies in Asia that he successfully
ran for twenty years before he married his current wife. She convinced
him to let go of the businesses and live with her in the UK. At the
time she was a headmistress in a school and was able to focus her
desire for control on the pupils. When she retired there was no one to
control other than John, and she switched her full attention to him.*

Now sixty-two, John was very miserable, and it was hard to believe that he had been such a dynamic person in the past.

After the first therapy session he stood up to his wife, and she left him. He was elated and felt a freedom in his heart for the first time in many years, as he was finally able to bring his art materials into the house. Previously he was only allowed to use the shed at the bottom of the garden, which had also been his refuge and where he had spent most of the day. Unfortunately, his son came to him and begged him to take his mother back, saying she was completely miserable, so he agreed. His wife quickly reestablished her pattern of control, but this time it was easier for him to tell her that she needed to resolve her personal control issues or leave.

John was Andy's client, and he illustrates why having boundaries and fortifying them is so important. Saying no to being controlled by someone else is imperative to keeping us aligned with the internal compass of our eternal soul and protects our physical, mental, and emotional states.

PERSONAL BOUNDARIES

To start building boundaries we have to notice how we feel when we give something to another person. We have to be honest with ourselves if we feel underlying resentment or irritation and then confront it head on. We have to say no to those who keep draining us.

Fear, guilt, and self-doubt are potential pitfalls of not creating boundaries. We may fear the other person's response to our boundaries and that the relationship may end as a result. Or we may anticipate feeling guilty if we stand up for ourselves and say no to loved ones or doubt that we even deserve to have boundaries. Sometimes, the belief is that we have to accept a situation because of cultural obligations, even if we are being drained, taken advantage of, or manipulated.

However, boundaries are a sign of a healthy relationship and self-respect. People who resonate and care for us will respect and understand our boundaries. People who do not resonate with us will react against them. In some cases, we may have to completely detach from them because they are in a different energy vibration from us.

When we permit ourselves to set and preserve boundaries, it will illuminate those who really resonate with and care for us. These are the people we can spend a lot of time with because they are healthy for us.

Creating Boundaries

Once you have decided to create a boundary, some people will understand it easily as it's innate. With others who have a different personality or cultural background, you may need to be very firm. Be respectfully assertive and let the other person know what is bothering you and how they can cooperate to address it. Make sure that you follow through with action so they take you seriously.

People are sometimes better at creating boundaries if a loved one is being impacted. Think of yourself as the loved one to create that strong boundary for yourself. Start with a small boundary that is not threatening. Then incrementally increase to the more challenging boundaries. Setting and sustaining boundaries is essential for healthy relationships.

If you are feeling uncomfortable in setting a boundary, seek support from those with whom you share mutually implicit trust. Those who are fully in resonance with you, and who you can talk to about your vulnerability. Sometimes the decision to create a boundary can have a big impact, so talking about it and getting support from someone who truly cares is important.

Maintaining Boundaries

There are two key red flags that indicate we are ignoring or letting go of our boundaries. The first is discomfort. This is a cue that a violation has been made or a boundary has been crossed. It is our intuition screaming a warning. The second is resentment. This occurs when we are pushing ourselves beyond our limits and feel that we are being taken advantage of and are not being appreciated or that someone is imposing their expectations or values on us.

Think of discomfort and resentment as being on a continuum from 1 to 10. If we are in the higher zones (6–10), we can ask, What is bothering me? and Is there an underlying emotion that I need to clear or a boundary that I need to reinforce? We also have to come to terms with the realization that sometimes detachment is the only strategy that works for those who repeatedly disrespect the boundary.

✧ Exercise: Creating Boundaries in Relationships

Record the following in your journal:

1. List the people who are a challenge to be with, or who you have difficulty saying no to.
2. For each person, identify any negative emotion they trigger and its intensity on a scale of 0 to 10, with 10 being the highest. For any level above a 5, do some emotion-reducing activities discussed in earlier chapters.
3. List the type of boundary you will create for each person.
4. Identify who will be in your support system to provide help when creating boundaries.
5. Write down the positive emotion you will experience once boundaries have been established and are working.
6. Add the positive emotion to this affirmation: "I feel (the emotion) now that I can create and manage my boundaries."

7. Place this affirmation somewhere you will read it daily to remind you of the boundary until it is no longer needed.

8. Create the boundary, sometimes in small steps if that helps. Just saying no to someone is the first big step.

Boundaries in the Old Consciousness

In 1924 when the Neva River in St. Petersburg flooded, the caged dogs of Russian physiologist Ivan Pavlov almost drowned in the water. Pavlov observed that the dogs were not the same afterward. They forgot their learned behaviors, and the fear from the event changed their dispositions. He later found he could condition his dogs by subjecting them to other types of stress as well as fear.

This was the start of a program in Russia that also moved to other parts of the world and led to the conditioning of humans,[1] which involved three steps. The first was to create stress through fear, sleep deprivation, or drugs. The second was to influence a subject's beliefs by constantly repeating new ideas or thoughts. And the third step was to separate the subject from different views.

These will be discussed shortly, but first let's look at some research by psychologist Stanley Milgram,[2] who wanted to explore how far people would go in following orders from those in authority. In one experiment, his subjects thought that they were administering electrical shocks to "learners" who failed to respond correctly. In reality, the learners were actually part of the research team. The experiment's subjects were told they would be operating a shock generator with gradations ranging from slight shock to severe shock.

Even when the learners acted as if they were experiencing clear signs of discomfort and distress, the majority of the subjects continued to follow instructions and administer shocks. It seems that people can very easily slip into a passive mode of following directions from those they see as being authority figures rather than taking personal responsibility for their actions. Some subjects, however, stopped partway through or refused to participate and said that although they felt pressure to continue, they were able to resist.

In the old consciousness, fear has been used as a tool for control and conditioning for thousands of years. When fear is combined with one message that is repetitively given, and alternative views are suppressed, it's like Pavlov's conditioning. And those in authority getting people to conform by using the social pressure of a situation is just like Milgram's research.

What is important to remember when embarking on the journey to the New Consciousness is to be very careful of the information and the energy we allow into our consciousness. We need to create a boundary against the information and energy from the duality and chaos in the old consciousness, particularly anything that can create fear. It can come from many sources, including mainstream or social media, emails, events, or people we know.

Once we identify the negative sources, we can consider greatly reducing our exposure to them or completely stopping them for a period and performing an information detox. During this time we can also use mindfulness activities that enable us to stay in the present moment, such as walking in nature, gardening, creating art, making crafts, or other similar activities. We can also look for sources of news and information that focus on oneness and cohesiveness because they will have a higher vibrational energy associated with them.

Awakening Neutrality and Embracing Uncertainty

When looking for the truth in information, we need to take a step back from political sides, polarities, and ideologies and maintain a sense of neutrality. Embracing uncertainty enables us to ask better questions. We can then act as a sacred scientist truly seeking to understand why something is happening without bias interfering with or stopping our inquiry.

Neutrality and uncertainty will help us explore what drives the world we live in. Moving beyond political sides or ideological thinking and ceasing to see our world as black and white is part of awakening neutrality. Developing a sense of empathy enough to wonder why something is happening or why someone does something is awakening neutrality.

With more neutrality we are able to embrace the idea of moving past stories, ideas, beliefs, and concepts we learned from the illusion of the old consciousness. As the illusion begins to move out of our mind and body, and we create space for new information that feels right in our hearts, we can imagine and develop possibilities for something new.

✦ Exercise: Setting Boundaries around Old Consciousness Information Sources

1. List all the sources of information about world events you use at the moment, including mainstream media and social media.
2. Identify which of those sources you will stop consulting and for how long, and what alternative activities you will take up to fill that time.
3. List possible alternative sources of news information.
4. Identify which alternatives to keep using neutrality, uncertainty, and what feels right in your heart.

SUMMARY OF CHAPTER 8

Our view of the world has been shaped in the past by others who control the narrative, often for their benefit, and held in place by fear and our beliefs. This is something we can change. Having personal boundaries and filtering the information coming to us enables us to control the information and the energy that we allow into our personal energy field. Embracing neutrality and uncertainty with this new information allows us to be the sacred scientist asking the right questions. The truth that we strive for will be guided by our hearts.

We can begin to see our world in a different way—building systems based on connection, cooperation, and equality rather than separation, competition, and dominance.

9

Listening to Our Soul Consciousness

You were born with wings, why prefer to crawl through life?
JALAL AL-DIN RUMI, THIRTEENTH-CENTURY SUFI

———————— ✧ ————————

Sometime after moving to our house in the country, we went away for a weekend and on arriving back found the attic full of bees, some dead and some trying desperately to get out against a glass window. Outside the house we noticed that a swarm of bees had made a home for themselves in the apex of the house and had been escaping through small cracks into the house. Unfortunately, the nest was an inaccessible place to have the swarm collected by local beekeepers, and we did not want to call in a pest exterminator. So, Reena used her intuition to communicate with the queen bee and tell her that it was not a good place to set up a hive and encouraged her to leave. Within twenty-four hours all the bees had left.

This could be put down to a coincidence, except the following year the same thing happened, and the bees left within twenty-four hours of Reena talking to the queen again. If humans have a consciousness extending outside the body, then the same can apply for animals, insects, and all things. And we can communicate with that consciousness if we open our mind to the possibility and have a sensitive intuition.

DIFFERENT TYPES OF INTUITION

Intuition is our instinct and is what we first feel or sense before the analytic mind becomes involved. In modern times intuition has been discredited and distrusted in preference for rational analytical thought and scientific evidence. However, intuition is the soft gentle whisper of our soul consciousness. Some people refer to it as a gut feeling. Many successful captains of industry use intuition for making important decisions when not all the information is available or when the information available is too confusing.

Sometimes it is hard to hear to the quiet messages of our intuition through the loud clattering thoughts in our head. Learning to hear, trust, and act on our intuitive impulses is a vital key to unlocking the deep power of the soul consciousness.

There are three different sources of intuition. The first is the subconscious mind. This is the large store of old information pushed below the level of conscious awareness. The second is the telepathic connections with people, animals, and nature we make when we tune in to their consciousness. The third is a connection to higher sources that gives us a spiritual perspective to look at choices differently.

Our soul consciousness sends us intuitive impulses through visions, sounds, or feelings or through knowing. Some of the ways we receive these impulses include:

+ Tingling or goose bumps
+ Lightheadedness or a strong energy flow in the chest

+ Heightened energy or a sense of abstraction
+ Repeated urges or a deep inner knowing
+ Signs and synchronicities in the external world supporting internal intuitive signals
+ Simple and clear messages that do not force or control our choices, but highlight a situation
+ Life opening up in ways that are unimaginable
+ Gut feeling

We need to be comfortable following intuitive impulses, particularly when they contradict what our analytical mind tells us. Intuition may take us out of our comfort zone to pull us down an unexpected route, so courage is needed. But this is the route to deeper wisdom and an authentic path leading to joy and fulfillment.

DEVELOPING INTUITION

Some people are born with a very strong intuition, on par with their rational mind. So it is very easy for them to pay attention to their intuitive impulses. However, most people have been conditioned to suppress their intuition in favor of their analytical skills, social conditioning or ingrained belief systems. For them, intuition is more intangible. The good news is that we never lose our intuitive skills. We can always develop our connection to our intuition and have clearer access to it.

Create a section in your journal where you can write down all your intuitive insights; carry it everywhere or review your day every evening and write down any insights you had earlier in the day. Your journal will contain a record of all events, even small ones, synchronicities, and intuitive insights and help you track your progress as your intuition develops.

Stilling the Mind

One way to improve our intuition is to reduce the effects of the mind and release the grip that our ego has on us. Trying to hear our intuition while our mind and ego chatter away is like trying to listen to a radio through the background hiss of static.

Stilling the mind can be achieved through walking in nature, reading books or poetry, listening to gentle music, or becoming fully absorbed in a physical activity, such as painting, yoga, craft activities, or gardening. What is important is staying mindful while we are doing the activity. For example, if you're walking in nature, focus on your feet touching the ground or the sounds and smells around you, or touch a tree and feel its texture. Focusing on a physical activity turns down the monkey chatter of the mind.

Meditation can also reduce the background noise of the mind and ego, allowing the intuitive information to become clearer. However, it needs to be done regularly and integrated permanently into our life.

✧ Exercise: Practicing Basic Meditation

Ten minutes of meditation a day is all that is needed to start to silence our mind and align our awareness. In the morning after we wake up is often the best time because the mind will be less active following sleep.

1. Find a sacred and quiet space where you will not be interrupted.
2. Sit upright with a straight spine and put all your focus on the breath as you breathe in and out.
3. Slow your breathing rate by breathing in for four seconds, holding your breath for four seconds, and breathing out for four seconds.
4. As you enter a relaxed state of meditation continue breathing naturally.
5. If you are aware of thoughts entering your mind during the meditation, remind yourself that the important part of you is not the thought. Be a distant observer and allow the thought to drift out of your mind

without adding energy by thinking about it. As you keep practicing, fewer thoughts will come up.

6. Keep a record in your journal about your meditation experience and how it changes over time.

Sometimes finding the right time for meditation can be a challenge. For example, John was a family man who found it difficult to meditate at home because of the demands of his children. His solution was to drive his car to a quiet spot in nature during his lunch break at work and do his meditation in the car. Whatever you decide works best for you, regular practice once a day is key.

Listening to Our Intuition

There are many fun ways to listen to our intuition. The exercises below are just a few examples.

◇ Exercise: Listening to Our Intuition through Cards

For this exercise you can use any type of cards with pictures. The more graphic the pictures the better. Our personal favorites are tarot cards that have colorful pictures with lots of detail.

1. Set your intention with the universe by asking a question on some topic that you want an answer to.

2. Shuffle the cards, pick one at random, and place it face up.

3. Look at the picture on the card and pay attention to the first thought to pop into your head that's connected to your question. If nothing happens, focus on part of the picture and see if that helps.

If you try this exercise too many times in succession, your concentration can waver. It's much better to practice it for a few minutes every day and believe that you can do it.

An alternative and fun way to do this is with a friend. One person takes the role of the client and asks a question aloud about some aspect of their life they want the cards to answer. The client shuffles the cards and draws out a card at random and lays it face down to represent the past. This is repeated with another card for the present and another one for the future.

The other person turns over the card representing the past, looks at the picture, and says the first thought that pops into their head, as this is likely to be the correct one. If no impressions come through, intuition can be stimulated by looking at part of the picture and again saying the first thing that pops in. This is repeated for the present and future cards.

The person who is playing the client can then do another past, present, and future reading with the cards and then compare it to the first reading of the other person.

✧ Exercise: Intuition with Letters and Phone Calls

Another method of practicing intuition is to try to sense the content of any letters you receive without opening them. Hold the envelope lightly between your fingers and press it to your forehead. See if you can feel what the letter is about. Or when you get a phone call, try to sense who is calling you before you answer.

The purpose of these exercises is not about accuracy but about allowing intuitive thoughts to emerge. Remember, intuition happens quicker than the analytic mind, so it is about learning to recognize the difference between intuition and the analytic mind. However, you may be delighted with the accuracy of the intuitive information and keep a record in your journal about your experiences.

SYNCHRONICITY

Synchronicity is a way that the universe communicates helpful information through timely unexpected events. It relies on your attention to what is going on around you in the outside world and how it relates to what your intuition is telling you or other events happening in your life.

I recall Simon, a successful manager in a large bank in Singapore, kept having intuitive thoughts to write a fictional book on past lives. He even had insights about what needed to go in the first book, but his well-paid job in the bank was so demanding the only way he could write a book would be to leave his job. But he had many financial commitments, including supporting children from previous relationships, and his wife had come from a childhood of poverty and was terrified of not being financially secure.

One day he decided to follow his intuition and resigned without warning his family. When he arrived home his twelve-year-old son came to him and said that if he ever lost his job, he would still love him. One week after leaving his job, Simon was approached by a colleague and offered employment that just met his financial needs but was not as time-consuming as the bank job, enabling him to start a writing career. He went on to write a series of books and for the first time found a deep spiritual contentment and knew he was on the right path in his life.

Simon was one of Andy's graduates. Notice the synchronicity of his son giving him a positive sign that it was okay to leave his job and a new job being unexpectedly offered that had the right balance of money and free time.

✦ Keeping Track of Synchronicities

Sometimes the whispers of the intuition are so quiet that it needs a synchronous event to get our attention. So, it is important to keep track of these events to understand the impact and implications to you. Journaling is the best way to do this. Set aside a section in your journal to record synchronic events and note how they relate to any messages you have received from your intuition or provide you with clues as to how to move forward in a particular situation.

INTUITIVE BLOCKS

We block our intuition when we do one or more of the following:

+ Banish our inner voices to follow cultural conditioning, belief systems, and trending news cycles
+ Allow our strong analytical mind to rule, which leads us to censor or disqualify intuitive experiences as luck, chance, or coincidence
+ Lead such a disorganized life that we fail to perceive obvious circumstances and higher insights in all the confusion
+ Become too busy and in too much of a hurry to perceive the whispers of our intuition, which needs stillness and quiet to be heard

The two most effective ways to unblock our intuition are opening our heart and accessing our wisdom.

An Open Heart Space

Opening our heart space increases our vitality and emotional balance. We become better communicators and more compassionate and in touch with both our own and others' needs.

A heart can be closed due to unresolved emotional issues or nagging worries and anxieties that lower our energy vibrations and deplete our energy. A closed heart is a typical response to pain, fear, and judgment. When we are personally triggered, our hearts and minds become fixated, and we become stuck. We go into protection mode to keep perceived threats at bay. When we close our heart, we believe the illusion that the threat and fear are real and retreat into learned helplessness. We also start making love conditional and using it as a currency, stifling its free flow.

The following exercises will help you keep your heart open.

✧ Exercise: Improving Our Heart Connection

1. Think of a loved one and remember a moment of laughter or joy with them. It does not need to be a big event, just one that makes you smile or feel joyful. This raises the energy vibration.
2. Fully connect with the event and recall the details that made this special as if it is happening now—it may even make you giggle or laugh out loud.
3. Send this energy you have created from your heart to the heart of the other person.

Make a list in your journal of the loved ones and happy experiences that give you joy and raise your vibration and keep a record of who or what you send this energy out to.

✧ Exercise: Getting Super Silly

Children have a naturally open heart space, so we can learn from them. Take time to be the silly, fun-loving child you once were before your parents, school, or culture changed you. Here are some possible activities that might help:

- Singing in the shower
- Walking barefoot in the rain
- Telling jokes
- Trying laughter yoga
- Connecting with the innocence and purity of seeing the world in wonderment
- Making changes in your life that lead you to new adventures

Record your experiences in your journal.

Our Innate Wisdom

Wisdom helps us align our outer and inner lives. It is a special knowledge that is both transcendent and transpersonal. It is not widely taught or accessible through left-brain learning.

To access our wisdom, we need to move beyond the thinking mind and our belief systems and see the world with an open mind. We can access wisdom by our inward focus and allowing answers to unfold intuitively from our eternal soul.

Disconnecting from the old beliefs that we have been conditioned with is difficult, but with perseverance and persistence, we can start to let go of them and with intuitive learning, we can reconnect to our deep wisdom within.

✧ Exercise: Connecting to Our Higher Wisdom

Many of the exercises on developing intuition are helpful in connecting with our higher wisdom. Writing with the nondominant hand is particularly useful. Art therapists have observed numerous people using this technique who have become more creative, expressive, and intuitive in their lives.[1]

1. Sit comfortably in a quiet setting and set the intention to be linked to your higher wisdom.
2. Ask about something that you want more spiritual information on, such as how to handle a difficult relationship or if a different type of work will give you more job satisfaction. Or you could ask if your energy protection is sufficient, what emotions you still need to clear, or if there are any life issues still to be mastered.
3. On a piece of paper begin to write freely with your nondominant hand. Do not lift the pen from the paper and be sure to write in cursive.
4. The alternative way to link to your higher wisdom is through meditation. Ask the question, still the mind, and wait for a thought or inspiration to come to you. Or ask a question before going to sleep and see what awareness you have about it in the morning.

Record your questions and answers in your journal.

✧ Exercise: Releasing Anything No Longer Serving You

Getting rid of clutter in our life frees up energy that enables the universe to fill it with something new and rewarding. Perhaps start by getting rid of clothes or personal items that are no longer needed, as this act symbolizes letting go of old relationships or beliefs that are no longer needed. Make a list of all the things you can release in your journal and then do it.

SUMMARY OF CHAPTER 9

Life is busy, and we are often in a rush to cross off items on our daily to-do lists. In order to listen to our intuition and bypass the mind and the grip our ego has on us, we need to prioritize the development of our intuition. We have to listen, listen, and listen some more within the silence. And then be open to what we receive. This is especially important when we are being asked to make significant decisions.

Our soul consciousness speaks to us in so many different quiet ways. The more we are open to the language of the soul, the more intuitive we become. Carry your journal everywhere and record your intuitive or synchronistic experiences. Just as learning to play the piano requires regular practice in order to develop skill, the same applies to our intuition. After six months, review your journal to ensure you have put in the required time and focus and if so, you will be amazed at how your intuition has developed.

10

Deepening the Connection with Our Soul Consciousness

Those who don't feel this Love
pulling them like a river,
those who don't drink dawn
like a cup of spring water
or take sunset like supper,
those who don't want to change,
let them sleep.

JALAL AL-DIN RUMI, THIRTEENTH-CENTURY SUFI

❖

There was a palpable feeling of disconnecting and shedding my ego self as my soul self rose to cross over. I shed how I had identified myself through work and social and cultural conditioning. They were not needed. There was a definite feeling of freedom and peace as I shed all the baggage of my ego and I expanded into my soul state. In the limited mindset of the ego everything mattered a great deal. In the expanded state of the soul very little mattered at all, which brought peace and freedom. I did not have to meet any standards. I just had to be me, making my choice.

The account on the previous page is Reena's description of the dropping away of the ego during her near-death experience and being in expanded soul consciousness.

SOUL CONSCIOUSNESS

Expanded soul consciousness happens in near-death experiences and also in between lives spiritual regression sessions. Many who had these experiences found their lives changed in the following ways:

+ Lowering or diminishing their anxiety and/or depression
+ Making them more open and receptive to life
+ Expanding their creativity and inspiration
+ Enhancing their intuition and personal gifts
+ Increasing their tolerance and patience
+ Giving them a greater mystical perception of life
+ Cultivating greater unconditional love
+ Losing their fear of death

Soul consciousness can also be experienced in other ways while being in our human body. It is a wise, unconditionally loving, creative wholeness and represents our most authentic state of being beyond our conditionings, fears, limiting beliefs, wounds, and ego fixations.

It helps us realize that the divine is right here inside each life breath, inside each heartbeat, inside everyone and everything around us. It makes us feel that there is a divine purpose, divine aim, divine ideal, and divine goal. Within soul consciousness, everything is constantly expanding and growing into higher and more fulfilling light.

EGO CONSCIOUSNESS

Ego consciousness is made up of limiting beliefs, judgments of others, unresolved emotional issues, imperfection, greed, and a lack of spiritual awareness. It seeks joy in earthly possessions and wants to remain here on Earth at all costs.

Ego consciousness tries to convince us that the divine is somewhere else, millions of miles away, and that we are nowhere near truth or fulfillment. It also makes us feel that we can exist without the divine.

When we are stuck in our ego consciousness, we might experience the following symptoms:

+ Being in conflict with others who have a different view
+ Believing we (or our work or ideas) are always better than others
+ Always wanting to win
+ Interrupting others a lot
+ Not acknowledging others' work or ideas
+ Not waking up excited in the morning
+ Having high highs and really low lows
+ Feeling that life that isn't entirely fulfilling anymore
+ Being surrounded by people who are bringing us down
+ Ignoring our dreams and feeling scared to move on
+ Working in a job that depletes us of energy
+ Stuck living in the rat race and not knowing our next step

TRANSCENDING FROM EGO TO SOUL CONSCIOUSNESS

We can transcend from ego consciousness to soul consciousness while we are in our current life. It will not be as quick or as intense as going through a near-death experience, but with consistent practice and conscious awareness of the tips and steps that are covered in this book, the transcendence to soul consciousness will occur.

We have come up with four steps to transcend our ego consciousness and move into soul consciousness while being embodied in our current incarnation:

1. Accepting and cleansing our shadow
2. Detaching
3. Shattering illusion
4. Being not doing

Accepting and Cleansing Our Shadow

Carl Jung created the idea of archetypes. He suggested that within each person there exists the persona and the shadow self.

The shadow self is an archetype that forms part of the unconscious mind and is composed of cultural conditioning, repressed ideas, instincts, impulses, weaknesses, desires, perversions, and embarrassing fears. This archetype is often described as the "darker side" of the psyche, representing wildness, chaos, and the unknown. Jung believed that this latent energy is present in all of us, in many instances forming a strong source of creative energy.

The persona, according to Jung, defines who we would like to be and how we wish to be seen by the world. The word *persona* is derived from a Latin word that literally means "mask" and can be used to represent all of the different social masks that we wear in different situations and among different groups of people.

The persona is the lovable face we present to the world, while the shadow is the face we hide from the world. When we are ashamed or embarrassed of our shadow, we are not accepting or unconditionally loving our whole self. Normally it is the ego that hides our shadow from the world.

Our ego represses our shadow selves due to a number of influences, including cultural conditioning and spirituality and religion.

Cultural Conditioning

Cultural conditioning happens all through our life. As young children our parents influence us, and we play with other children and adapt to their way of behaving. Also affecting us are the schools we attend, our relationships, our working environments, and our relatives, friends, and colleagues.

Some cultural conditioning can be very strong, such as in the case of Ashtiaq Asghar reported by the BBC.[1] Ashtiaq lived in the UK and came from a traditional Muslim family who were planning an arranged marriage for their son with a girl from Pakistan. They would have been horrified to learn he was dating a white girl named Laura, so he made her keep their relationship a secret. She fell pregnant as a result of a fling with another man and had a daughter. Still dating Ashtiaq, she became tired of keeping his secret and made the fatal mistake of revealing it to his family. He asked Laura to meet him by the canal one evening and murdered her to avoid shame on the family.

Some cultural conditioning is less obvious, as Andy experienced when he took an assertiveness course when he was younger and working in business. He was surprised to discover how uncomfortable it was for him to use the words *I want*. He had always used other phrases such as *could you* or *will you*. On mentioning it to his sister he discovered that she could not use this phrase either and realized that when they were children their parents had often said, "I wants don't get," so the I want phrase had been conditioned out of him.

We live in a judgmental world. Becoming and fitting in to civilized society requires us to repress aspects of ourselves that do not fit with the structured ideal of our society. We are born whole and complete, but we slowly learn to live fractured lives, accepting some parts of our nature but rejecting and ignoring other parts to please our parents, to be accepted by our friends, and to find and keep work. The media plays a huge part in creating culture, so we repress what the media considers to be "shadow" to fit in to society in general. The repression of negative traits or emotions is one of the biggest barriers in any person's journey toward self-love and authentic living.

And, as Reena found out while she was going through her near-death experience, society's and other people's acceptance means very little at the end:

There was no one with me as I crossed over. Nobody knew I was dying. I could not tell anyone. That transcendental journey was something I went through by myself. The light beings who greeted me and told me it was my time to die did not judge my choices. They simply presented the information, understood my decision, and let me come back into my body. So then I wondered why I was so ashamed of the parts of myself that I hid from the world. All these judgments from other egos and agendas mean nothing at the end, so why should they mean something in life? So one of the major decisions I made when I came back was to resonate me . . . all of me. Those who share the same resonance with me will come and stay with me, and those who do not will fall away. It is better to have a small circle of people who truly see and love me the way I am, both shadow and persona, than to twist myself into a pretzel to fit into a bigger community that brings only emptiness and feelings of worthlessness. The best decision I made was to continue living my life in peace and freedom.

Spirituality and Religion

Modern spiritual and religious beliefs revolve around moving toward the Light (or God) or being good. Many spiritual and religious movements have principles that we must adhere to, to be in the light, while completely ignoring or condemning the darker elements because they are associated with negativity or evil. What is a shame is that the structures that uphold the value of practicing unconditional love also hold dualistic ideologies of light and dark, good and bad. When spirituality and religion hold principles of duality, then people who adhere to the beliefs will also avoid what is considered to be dark, or bury it deeper within them, to fit in to the spiritual or religious circle.

The following is an extract from a past life review during a between lives spiritual regression. Notice that there is no judgment of right or wrong, just questions to enable deeper insight and suggestions of alternative ways of managing difficult situations.

I need to go and discuss what's happened. . . . My spirit guide, he's standing with his arms crossed, shaking his head. I'm like the little pupil and he's the teacher. He's got a long beard and a long white gown. He's full of love and warmth, but at the same time he's strict. He's been my guide for a number of lives now. . . . It's more than telepathy, it's feelings as well, it's everything. I can see inside his mind and he can see inside mine, except he can keep certain things from me. I'm still learning how to do that. . . . He's asking me why I always take the easy way out. I have a problem with facing problems. He tells me I need to stop thinking about things so much. I need to just learn to live, instead of being so introverted. I need to experience the world around me, rather than just experiencing the world within me. I'm my own worst enemy. Whatever I feel inside me, I project onto the world around. Most situations aren't as bad as they seem, but I seem to make them harder. . . . He knows I need to have a rest for a bit and he's projecting love as well.

A Balanced Self

To take responsibility for ourselves and completely experience unconditional self-love, we must learn to honestly face and accept our shadow selves. This is not about indulging the shadow but acknowledging and taking responsibility for it. Once we truly acknowledge these shadow traits instead of avoiding them, they will suddenly stop having control over us. Then we can choose: Do we wish to keep our shadow or do we wish to work on letting it go?

A whole and balanced self is a reconciliation of all parts, an inner unification. To accept and unconditionally embrace our shadow self is to become whole again and thus taste a glimpse of what authentic wholeness feels like. This is the way we stop fearing. When we accept, like, and love our wholeness, it does not matter what others say. We will see judgments for what they are and not take them personally. All we have to do is be true to our whole being, and our vibrations will draw others to us who resonate in the same way. We will also be more likely to see everyone around us as whole beings, and with understanding and unconditional love rather than condemnation and judgment.

Illuminating and Acknowledging Our Shadow

Illuminating and acknowledging our shadow takes courage and bravery. Our ego will be terrified to show that perceived dark part of ourselves for fear we will be rejected by society or ourselves. Illuminating and acknowledging our shadow may make us feel vulnerable, but it is the first step to setting us free from suffocating belief systems, and we can be strong in our vulnerabilities.

Here are some exercises for illuminating and acknowledging your shadow.

✧ Exercise: Meditating

1. Set an intention to see your shadow in silent meditation for 15 to 30 minutes a week.

2. Be gentle, receptive, and compassionate. It is important to not be judgmental of your shadow self.

3. Let the different shadow parts reveal themselves one by one—give it time.

4. It is important not to reframe your shadow parts as light or make excuses for them. That is ego talking. Just let them emerge and sit with them.

5. Once you are comfortable with these shadow parts, you can decide how to take responsibility for them—do you wish to transform them or keep them with love because they resonate with your current vibration?

6. You can develop more self-awareness by becoming more conscious of your words, thoughts, feelings, and behaviors, which will allow you to take responsibility for your shadow self.

✧ Exercise: Drawing or Painting

An effective way to understand yourself is through art—by drawing or painting whatever you are feeling or thinking.

1. Get a blank piece of paper, find a quiet place, and turn your attention inward.

2. Ask your shadow, What do you want me to know right now? and then paint or draw whatever comes to mind. Even the strangest mental images or scenarios can hold a seed of wisdom, helping to reveal hidden feelings, thoughts, or memories.

3. Be sure to approach this activity nonjudgmentally and with an open mind. If you fear judgment from yourself, you may feel inhibited and may not be able to benefit fully from this practice. So you should be gentle and receptive, allowing whatever wants to arise, to arise. Remember that our shadow is a part of us, but it does not define us.

✧ Exercise: Journaling

1. Every day for a few weeks keep a record in your journal of both good and bad emotions, thoughts, and habits. This practice will help shine a light on the brighter and darker elements of your nature.

2. Read through your journal entries periodically to recover the balance you need in your life, accepting both light and dark parts of yourself.

3. When you do so, be sure to adopt an analytical, nonjudgmental, and compassionate attitude toward yourself, rather than playing the role of the prosecutor, judge, or defendant, which will hinder your ability to embrace your shadow self fully.

✧ Exercise: Contacting Your Spirit Guide

Use your nondominant hand for connecting with your spirit guide as mentioned in previous chapters. Set the intention to be linked to your guide and ask for information about your shadow side. For instance, I would like my spirit guide to give me information about my shadow side. On a piece of paper begin free writing the answer with your nondominant hand.

Do not be shackled by your shadow parts. Illuminate and integrate them, or illuminate and let them go.

Detaching

The following is from the Council of Beings of Light:

> Because of fear people attach themselves to people or things or concepts. A concept is not tangible and the amount of energy put into it makes it a reality. It varies in different parts of the world, but a big concept is the need for money. Earth was created with abundance, with enough for everyone, and yet the concept is that money is needed for survival. And people physically struggle with stress and illness for it. Another one is the attachment to people and sadness when they pass away. Some go into despair, and yet it is just the cycle of life.
>
> At the end of the day it is all about energy and none can possess it, and it is an energy accessible to all. Just let go of all attachment to possessions. This thing that is seen as impor-

tant is not. The vibration of money does not equate with energy. It does not equate with the beauty of nature. And you have Mother Earth energy on your side and all on the side of the light. Let go of the attachment of possession. Possession is weighty, burdensome, and heavy.

Ali ibn Abi Talib, who Muhammad called his guardian and successor, said, "Detachment is not that you should own nothing, but that nothing should own you." When we become too attached to something, it becomes a major part of our ego selves and our identity. That is not necessarily a bad thing because we still need to have that attachment to be motivated and driven to fulfill our purpose. The danger is in letting attachment and ego become all of who we are. When our attachments become all we are, we link our behavior, our performance, our productivity, and our self-worth to that limited egoic attachment, disregarding our whole self.

Reena experienced this firsthand during her near-death experience when she split from and shed her egoic self:

When my ego split from my soul consciousness and dropped away, what dropped away with it were my attachments to my work and conditioned labels. Before my near-death experience, I was concerned about how many books would sell because I had tied my identity to the success of my work and measured that with the number of sales. The freedom I felt when I detached from that while my ego split from my soul self is immeasurable. It felt like a huge burden that I had put on myself had fallen away, releasing me from its heavy, limiting bind. My identity is not measured by any ego achievements or labels. When I detached, I found my real soul identity, which I brought back with me, and I found my peace.

Some level of attachment to an external anchor gives us a sense of self-worth, which makes us likely to be highly productive. So the solution is not to detach completely. It is simply to recognize when we are so attached to something that it owns us.

We were in the Maldives, and as Reena observed fish and sea creatures swimming freely, she wondered why humans have caged themselves into systems so that they have no freedom to move. There was a time when all creatures were free to move and eat. Although there was always the cycle of life, and it was tough to survive, it was also possible to thrive. Unfortunately, that is not so much the case now, and it has not been for a long time. Much of our lack of freedom has to do with our attachment to the people and things in our life.

When we are faced with loss, grief, or failure, unhealthy attachment leads to emotional and mental pain and affects our mental health. In these cases, detachment can move us out of acute suffering and into something close to peace.

Yet we cannot leapfrog into detachment. That's why the Bhagavad Gita recommends developing our detachment muscles by working on them day by day, starting with the small things.

Our ego will fight hard to prevent us from making any changes, so to break the hold of the ego and embrace our soul consciousness we need to slowly begin to replace these thoughts. Detachment takes practice and it reveals itself in the following five stages:

1. *Acknowledgment:* When there is something we want, we can begin by recognizing it and then feeling how much we want it. Or if we are experiencing the hopelessness of actual loss, we need to allow it in.

2. *Self-inquiry:* In meditation, we can explore the energy of the feeling of the desire or hopelessness of the loss and be present with it, but stand a little aside from it. Then we need to

let it out so that it does not fester within. Journaling, talking to a trusted, supportive person, or even breathing out the emotions (if they are not too heavy) will work. Sometimes, a therapist will be needed if the emotions are too heavy.

3. *Processing:* When you process the desire or loss you realize that you have actually gained something, even if it is just a lesson in what not to do in the future. One of the reasons to take time processing the desire or the loss is that when we do act, we are not paralyzed by fear or driven by the frantic need to do something (anything!). It helps us convince ourselves we have some degree of control. So we can choose a deliberate response as opposed to reacting.

4. *Creative action:* Loss or desire can paralyze us so that we find ourselves without the will to act or else we act in meaningless, ineffective ways. In the early stages of loss or in the grip of strong desire, it is sometimes better just to do the minimum for basic survival. As we move forward in the processing, ideas and plans will start to bubble up and we will feel actual interest in doing them. This is when creative action can be taken.

5. *Freedom:* This is a state of true liberation, a feeling of putting down a heavy burden. It is a big achievement.

Every time we free ourselves from one of those sticky attachments, we unlock another link in what the yogi texts call the chain of bondage, which frees us to embody our soul consciousness.

✧ Detaching from Desire or Loss

Whether we're doing it daily or as a way of dealing with a big challenge practicing detachment is easier if we do it with a soft attitude.

1. Connect to the Soul Consciousness, and then offer up to the Universe whatever we are doing, whatever we intend or want, or whatever

we try to get free of. (That's the time-honored method set forth in the Bhagavad Gita: Offer the fruits of your labor to God.)

- Offering our actions helps train us to do things not for any particular gain or personal purpose but simply as an act of praise or gratitude, or as a way of joining our consciousness to the greater Consciousness. Offering our desires, fears, and doubts loosens the hold they have on us, reminding us to trust in the Universe—the source of both our longings and their fulfillment.

2. Once you've done this, bring to mind the action you're about to do or the outcome required.

3. Mentally make an offering of it to the Universe.

   - You can say something like, "I offer this to the source of all, asking that it be accomplished in the best possible way."

   - If your issue is a strong attachment or something that disturbs you about yourself, your life, or someone else, bring it to mind and offer that. You might say, "May there be balance and harmony in this situation," or "May things work out for the benefit of all," or "May things work out according to the highest good."

4. If you care deeply about what you're offering—your desire for a particular relationship, or your wish for the well-being of yourself or of someone you love—you may notice that you're reluctant to let go of it. If that's the case, offer it again. Keep offering it until you feel a loosening of your identification with your hope, fear, desire, anger, or feeling of injustice. Whenever you feel the clutch of attachment, offer it again.

5. Once you've made the offering, let yourself linger in the feeling space you've created inside yourself. The nurturing force of your soul energy is the only power that really dissolves fears and attachments. The more we get to know that vast, benign energy, the more we realize it is the source of our power and love. And that's when our detachment becomes something greater—not detachment from desire or fear but

awareness that what we are is so large, it can hold all of our smaller feelings inside itself and still be completely free.

Shattering Illusion

Shattering illusion is something that Reena experienced during her near-death experience:

> As my ego detached and dropped away, I was struck by how much of what I viewed as important was not. Happiness is found in the simple things in life that we take for granted. Just sitting with my family made my soul sing. Eating something delicious made my soul sing. Being with people who really resonate with me made my soul sing. Before my near-death experience I used to live to work because in the illusionary world my ego had built, achieving success in that arena made me happy. After my near-death experience, I realized that it did not matter from my soul perspective. My soul did not care . . . yet I ignored my soul and my health to fulfill an illusion.

The following are examples of the many limitations of illusion:

+ *Limitation of attachment:* Attachment creates the thought, *I need this to be complete in some way.* When we trust that every moment is complete in itself, we step into the freedom of life. The sun rises, the sun sets—it's impossible to hold on to the day or night. Enjoy what comes and be at peace with what doesn't.
+ *Limitation of knowledge:* The need for knowledge leads us to believe, "I know this, but I don't know that." By tapping into the field of infinite possibilities, we access a state of all-knowing, where everything exists as pure potential waiting to be enlivened by our intention.

♦ *Limitation of fear:* The illusion that there is something to be afraid of is perhaps the most insidious of all. The illusion of fear is the tool used by people to manipulate and control others to fall in line with personal agendas. Very little can harm us except the shadows we create within the ego. The soul consciousness is eternal and cannot be harmed.

When we become ensnared in the illusions of the ego, we suffer. All suffering is a result of our ego living a life of doubt, confusion, pain, and frustration. We can choose to live the true qualities of life when we transcend the ego consciousness and move into soul consciousness, expanding our view of reality and effortlessly moving beyond the illusion. We can transcend the worldly limitations and step into the wisdom of the unlimited unknown.

✧ Exercise: Shattering Illusions

1. In your journal, make a list of limiting beliefs you hold on to that prevent you from living life to its fullest. These are the excuses and illusions we create for ourselves that block our spiritual progress, such as I'm too old, I'm too small, I'm not smart enough, I'll never be enlightened.

2. Sit quietly in meditation and ask yourself, What are these illusions, these limitations that are preventing me from doing things? Where did they come from and what do they provide for me? Then release them in whatever way is comfortable. Journaling can be used. Or perhaps visualize blowing it out into a balloon and releasing the balloon into the sky.

3. Pause and simply be aware of your breath. Illusions take you into the past or the future, but the real you is in the NOW. Your breath is always in the present, so when you focus on it, it will bring you into the present as well.

4. Check with your soul consciousness by seeing what you are doing or feeling is resonant. Illusions will make your chest clench, stomach

feel uncomfortable, and mind anxious, filled with worrying thoughts. What resonates with your soul consciousness will fill you with passion, lightness, joy. Find what resonates with your authenticity, your light, periodically throughout the day. It is your truth and purpose, and you should live it. The path that is shown by your light is the only path that is right for you.

Being Not Doing

The job of the ego mode of mind is to get things done, to achieve particular goals. Once the ego becomes involved, it is much more difficult to simply let go of the goals we have set. We feel forced or obligated to do things, which leads to our mind not being in the present experience. It is so preoccupied with analyzing the past or anticipating the future that the present is given a low priority. Our only interest in it is to monitor whether we have succeeded or failed in meeting our goals. So we find ourselves in the prison of our mind and obligations, which leads us away from peace.

Being is a state that takes us back to simple existence. It is characterized by direct, immediate, intimate experience of the present, allowing us to be fully aware of whatever is here, right now. The focus of being is accepting and allowing what is, without any immediate pressure to change it. Allowing arises naturally when there is no goal or standard to be reached and no need to evaluate experience to reduce discrepancies between actual and desired states.

When we are just being, thoughts and feelings are seen as simply passing events in the mind. Emotions do not immediately trigger old habits of action in the mind or body directed at hanging on to pleasant feelings or getting rid of unpleasant emotions. There is a sense of freedom and freshness as experience unfolds in new ways. The state of existing, the most important or basic part of a person's mind or self, enables us to stop for a minute and consider our direction.

Doing involves thinking about the present, the future, and the past, relating to each through a veil of concepts. The ego mind often travels forward to the future or back to the past, and the experience is one of not actually being here in the present much of the time. The mind seeks to achieve the goals to which doing is dedicated. Feelings are primarily evaluated as good things to hang on to or bad things to get rid of. Our wonderful multidimensional complexity of experience is boiled down to a narrow, one-dimensional focus—our goals. Through the act of trying to make certain things happen, we may lose track of the big picture of our lives.

When we are being, we are:

- Connecting with the present moment
- Acknowledging how things are in the moment
- Willing to allow things to be just as they are with no effort to change experience
- Open to and accepting of pleasant, neutral, and negative emotional states
- Calm and still, with a sense of being centered

When we are doing, we are:

- Focusing on how things are and how they "should" be
- Making goal-oriented efforts to fix things
- Struggling harder to reach our goals
- Acting automatically and paying little attention to our intuition
- Lacking conscious awareness of the present moment

Breaking away from the egoic doing and acquiring the state of being requires work and intuition. However, there are many benefits to reaching the state of being that make the effort worthwhile:

+ Being gives us more time than doing. Identifying the really important tasks based on our intuition enables us to concentrate our efforts on the things that really matter to us.

+ Being doesn't require any special knowledge and is much easier than doing. We only need to let go and relax; the rest will come naturally when we are in the flow. This might take practice, but you don't need any special knowledge to do it.

+ Being uses less energy than doing. When we are doing, we exert our energy to achieve something. When we are in a state of relaxed being, we use less energy and can easily recharge.

+ Being increases our personal development. When we are in a calm reflective state, we get in touch with ourselves. This leads to greater awareness and furthers our growth in life.

+ Being is more fun than doing. When we are too busy doing, we miss experiencing the things that really make us happy. Being makes us aware of the most important things we have in our life and gives us more time to enjoy them.

All other animals seem happy just to exist. Humans, on the other hand, are not content just to be, they have to do something or achieve something. The ego drive produces a culture, belief system, and conditioning that imprisons us. The ego uses the will to work against the body by ignoring the feelings and warning messages the body sends out. Many people try to change themselves by using willpower to keep striving to reach their goals regardless of the negative effect it has on their health. True physical, mental, and emotional health can only be gained through self-awareness, self-acceptance, and the ability to rest, contemplate, and just be.

The ego works by setting a goal and controlling the actions to achieve it. Doing involves carrying out seemingly productive activities that our mind thinks we need to do to give us what we think will bring happiness and success. Eventually it leads to an empty negative feeling of frustration and an uncomfortable yearning for something more substantial, positive, and real.

There is nothing intrinsically wrong with the doing mode. This approach has worked brilliantly as a general strategy for solving problems and surviving in the impersonal, external world. But life takes place on the balance point between making it happen (doing) and taking it as it comes (being), and it is all about getting the right balance between the two. In our culture today, too much emphasis is placed on doing and not enough on being. Coming back to being and moving from ego to align with soul consciousness will help us find a love of self and of life, deep joy, and peace.

✧ Exercise: Being and Doing

1. In your journal, make a list of all the things that you typically do every day and see if there are any you can do less frequently or stop doing altogether.
2. Make a list of the different ways of being you can do in a typical day.

HOPE

Hope is the life force that keeps us going and is a crucial part of dealing with life's problems and maintaining resilience. Hope is directly related to our sense of possibility. The greater our perception of possibilities, the greater our hope. The ego consciousness is very limited. Therefore, transcending our ego and moving into our expanded soul consciousness will give us more hope.

Hope is not the same as happiness or optimism. It is what we feel when we think that life is worth living, that our work is worth doing. Hope is what we have when we have a positive relationship with our existence. When we begin to lose hope things can seem bleak. When we run into constant resistance and are prevented from reaching our goals, we can start to feel like there is nothing to live for. So maintaining hope through embodying our soul consciousness will lead us to feel much happier about life. It will let us see the abundance and beauty in life and will allow us to enjoy the experience of living on Earth.

LIVING AUTHENTICALLY

There will always be people who think that what you are doing is wrong. We all have conditioned ideas about how we should behave, what kind of things we should and should not do, what kind of job we should have, and so on. Those who are living authentically, from their soul consciousness, will be able to listen to people around them without being thrown off course by criticism or questioning. They are tuned in to their own center and that is what leads and directs them. It is liberating when free from outside opinions and pressures, while following what resonates deeply from within. This is the secret of living authentically, living our truth.

Those who are living in their truth can openly and honestly listen to others without being defensive and fully hear what they have to say. They tend to be more interested in getting to know the person who they are speaking with as a unique individual rather than needing to justify their own opinions and thoughts based on what the other person is saying.

There is no need to agree with others to feel secure. Be happy to agree or disagree. Others are living their lives from their internal compass, and truth can be very individual and subjective. Those who are living authentically will ask for help when they need it and will take the opinions of those they respect into consideration, but at the end of the day they'll make their own choices. They'll take what they have heard and then tune in to themselves and choose from within.

Those being authentic will understand that they always have a choice and that anything that happens to them in their lives is based on the choices that they made. They also understand that they can choose how they react to what others do. They never play the victim card because they understand that they are sovereign, and it is no one else's job to do anything for them. They steer their own ships and make no excuses for what happens.

Authentic people understand that getting their needs met is not something to apologize for. They understand that when living in a world with others one needs to approach life with compassion and respect for all, and they understand how to create an environment around themselves where they can get their needs met in a way that is most harmonious for everyone. There is always a way to get things done peacefully, and that is how an authentic person meets their needs. They also understand that sacrificing themselves for other people doesn't really help anyone. A battery has to be charged to function. In the same way, authentic people understand that they have to recharge and reserve energy for themselves to be able to function.

Those who are walking in their truth fully understand that one cannot give from an empty cup. They take time every day to get their cups filled by doing the things they know nurture and replenish them. They never feel guilty for taking care of themselves because they understand that they are as valuable and worthy of love and attention as anyone else and that they are more effective givers when they have what they need.

They also take time every day to tune in to themselves. This is one of the biggest things that sets those who are living in their truths apart from those who are not. When you are walking in your truth, you are taking time every single day to pause and check in with yourself. You cannot walk in your truth if you do not know what your truth is. Spending time in quiet contemplation of some sort every day sets up a truth-based life.

Finally, those who are living in their truth are gracious and compassionate toward everyone else—whether the person they are interacting with is also living their truth or not. They understand that everyone is on their own unique journey and that judgment and condemnation of others really does not help anyone. Because authentic people are so secure in what they are doing, they tend to be naturally less judgmental of what others are doing. You will feel a sense of welcoming and acceptance when you are around an authentic person.

SUMMARY OF CHAPTER 10

Deepening our connection to our soul consciousness will be a different journey for everyone. This chapter introduced some ideas and tips to help you get there. The first task is to identify the things we are doing that come from our ego consciousness rather than soul consciousness. This can be challenging because our ego often creates blind spots, which in the busy acts of doing we never notice. Then we move on to identify the steps of accepting and cleansing our shadow, detaching, shattering illusion, and concentrating on being not doing.

When we are in our soul consciousness, it's easier to live in authenticity, be less judgmental of others, and be free to find real happiness.

11

Creating a New Earth through Our Soul Consciousness

As more people become aware of who they truly are, more will become willing to help the Earth repair itself. It is difficult to influence those who choose to forget and don't want to realize the damage they are causing through their greed, and this is why past civilizations chose to end themselves. There has to be some sort of multinational disaster or occurrence of some sort to enable this shift to take place. . . . But it hasn't been finalized, and it won't be a total disaster as in the past. . . . And afterward, those who remain in the physical will be aware of who they really are, while those souls who choose not to move forward will not reincarnate in the new experiment.

THE SPIRITUAL ELDERS,
EXPLORING THE ETERNAL SOUL

———————— ✧ ————————

A NEW CONSCIOUSNESS AND
A NEW EARTH

Channelings have told us that at the start of the transition from the Age of Pisces to the Age of Aquarius, two consciousnesses will coexist on Earth, the old and the new. Eventually, everyone who decides to stay on Earth will embrace the New Consciousness, but the speed in which this will happen is not clear.

There are some general principals to help us understand the journey. First it is not possible to design the world of the New Consciousness while we are still rooted in the old one. The New Consciousness will be created from the bottom up rather than the top down. This means not to expect governments or leaders from the old consciousness to do it, everyone will by working collectively together. There will be many creative ways to ground and apply the expanded consciousness and this evolution will happen in an organic way.

Once people are in the New Consciousness, they will quickly adjust to it, and they will never go back to the old consciousness way of living. Until then, there is much of value to be taken from the old consciousness, and everyone needs to decide where the boundary between the two exists.

The intent of the New Consciousness is to imagine and create a future that will generate the kind of community that people will want to be part of—one filled with the expanded consciousness of love, joy, and peace.

THE ONENESS OF
THE NEW CONSCIOUSNESS

The multinational disasters mentioned in the Spiritual Elders quote above can be seen in the chaos around us now and the breakdown of the old systems. Hidden truths are surfacing about the greed and corruption of those controlling multinationals and governments. This is to wake us up out of the illusion. We will then have the free will to choose to expand our consciousness and move to the Oneness of the New Consciousness, like the unwavering peace that Reena felt in her near-death experience or stay in the old consciousness.

The Oneness of the New Consciousness is the realization that we are all connected, so it is natural to move from an individual focus to one of helping others. Everyone is considered an equal yet we have our own purpose that we follow from our heart and with a strong intuition. Life becomes an adventure of joy and growth with no good or bad, just different consequences.

But Oneness is not necessarily drama-free. We can still express our different views or disagree with each other but without being gripped by the force of emotions. If a negative emotion is triggered, rather than suppressing it, we can allow it to surface and be released. After a disagreement, avoid reliving it in your mind so that you do not re-create the energy, which can cling to your thoughts. Staying with the thoughts that created a negative emotion will refuel it, and maintaining fear, sadness, hate, or anger energies is not helpful and will lower your vibration.

The good news is that a thought cannot sustain its energy, unless it's constantly fueled. The natural state is for the thought to release its acquired energy when it is not getting any new fuel. So after you release the emotion, become centered and then bring in the energies of love, happiness, and peace. The other person will feel your freeness, and this energy can help to defuse the argument or situation.

And Oneness does not necessarily mean that we become all-loving in terms of our thoughts—we may still have thoughts of like and dislike—but it helps us to accept that everything around us has a divine plan even if we do not know what it is.

It is also helpful to know what is going on within ourselves, and when we separate that from the illusions of what may seem to be true or what others may think, we are free. And being able to see what is truly happening and knowing what we are really feeling helps us to gain awareness, and awareness leads to staying awake and to a fulfilling life.

✧ Exercise: Being in Oneness

1. As any remaining shadow parts reveal themselves in your life day by day, know that this is natural. Center yourself when they appear, and if they persist, use the methods discussed in earlier chapters to dispel them.
2. On a daily basis, set the intention to break all energetic links with the old consciousness and then connect with the Oneness and ask for the energy to flow into your heart.
3. Set the intention to release the Oneness energy from your heart to radiate into the world at a vibration in the highest interest of all those you meet or the nature you encounter.

WEAVING IN THE ONENESS

From the Cocreators of Oneness:

> We are about dancing and creating the One. We do not dance and create for the One, we dance and create the One. The Oneness that holds it all together, that creates the fabric of consciousness, and we dance and create and weave the threads with our vibration. We weave this vibration through different souls through whom we speak, who go through a big transformation, especially in this period.
>
> But it has been accumulating over a number of years when the Divine Mother chose living in the Oneness, the new Oneness being created by the Council of Beings of Light who

are shaking up the old fabric of consciousness, and we bring in the new. So we work closely, as we are all brothers and sisters.

We come to talk about weaving the new Oneness. Weaving the new Oneness is about disconnecting yourself from the old consciousness. Anything that is of the old, anything irrelevant to the new, anything that is stale and stuffy that weighs you down needs to be discarded to start weaving the fabric of the New Consciousness.

So we wish to impart to you the discipline that can be used to disconnect from the old consciousness—anything or anyone. But you have to be ready to do this, and what or whom will fall away from you will be quite a surprise.

✧ Exercise from the Cocreators of Oneness: Weaving in the Oneness

Every morning before you get out of bed it is best to do this meditative practice. It is a vibrational meditation practice where you focus on disconnecting yourself from the old consciousness, which means cutting all the cords to mental, emotional, physical, and material attachments, and proceeding forward into the new. You will feel a vibrational difference, which is lighter, freer, higher, and you can breathe. The old consciousness is heavy and weighs you down. Cut as many cords as you can and step into the New Consciousness. See it as a bright light on the horizon and infuse yourself in the New Consciousness. Once you have infused yourself, weave the New Consciousness and dance with the Oneness.

Just know that this weaving can be put into every aspect of your lives. Be it brushing your teeth or communicating to people. Let go of anyone and anything that weighs you down. Let it go. The more you discard the more the souls that do not resonate will slip away. And fill your heart with the excitement and joy of the Oneness. We all are one—man, trees, creatures, planet. Dance with the Oneness, and start living in Oneness. We look forward to weaving and dancing in the Oneness with you.

GRATITUDE

Practicing gratitude is a powerful way to maintain the energy vibrations of the New Consciousness and bring warmth into our heart. Sarah Ban Breathnach, in her book *Simple Abundance*,[1] talks about appreciating the simple things in life and their abundance by keeping a daily gratitude journal that you write in every evening. The positive energy it creates filters to the subconscious and is held through the night. This raises our vibration and helps us to see the positive side of any situation we find ourselves in.

Robert Emmons, a professor of psychology at the University of California and an expert in using gratitude,[2] says that gratitude also helps us recognize the sources of goodness outside ourselves. This is when we acknowledge that other people or higher powers have given us many gifts and help in our lives and how we have been supported by them.

Research has shown that gratitude, like optimism, is associated with lower heart rate and blood pressure, better sleep quality, less stress, more positive expectations and reflections, and greater feelings of appreciation toward others.[3]

Gratitude can be thought of as a muscle that we can develop over time as we learn to recognize the abundance and gifts that we did not previously consider important.

✧ Exercise: Practicing Gratitude

1. At night before you go to bed, write five new things that you are grateful for in your journal. These can be simple or small things that you have previously taken for granted, such as the food you eat, the

sounds of nature, or living in a warm home, and they can include anything you achieved during the day that you are grateful for, such as making something work, showing love toward another person, or creating something new.

2. After a week or so, read through the pages of your journal and review the reasons you are appreciative of yourself and what the universe has given you. Writing them down and reading them at a later date makes them real and easier to acknowledge.

MANIFESTATION

One of the most exciting aspects of moving into the New Consciousness is to create the world that we would like to live in. We are leaving the old consciousness, detaching from illusions and what doesn't resonate with ourselves. But what are we moving to? We have to create that and manifestation is the best way to do this.

When we were moving into our new house, we noticed a neighbor's teak outdoor table and chairs. We both said that they would be perfect for an empty space at the rear of the new house and then returned our focus to unpacking. A little later that day we had a knock on the door, and we opened it to a man who said he had a set of new outdoor teak table and chairs for sale and was drawn to the house. Also, he was offering them at a discounted price. We immediately bought them and were full of gratitude to the universe.

While this is a simple example, it illustrates the principal of manifestation. The universe is full of abundance, and we are eternal beings that can create the environment around us for our spiritual learning. We do this through the life we plan as souls and the energy we project out to the universe through our thoughts and feelings.

Some things are easier and quicker for the universe to provide than others. For instance, a friend who moved to a self-sustaining community needed a house to live in. So instead of asking for the money to buy a house, he asked the universe for a home near the community. Shortly afterward he was asked to look after a house in return for living there just needing to pay the house bills until the owner came back. That was ten years ago, and there has been no sign of the owner since.

But suppose we ask for a winning million-dollar lottery ticket. If it does not arrive, it might be easy to dismiss the power of manifestation altogether. But some things like winning the lottery are difficult for the universe to arrange because they have aspects of future uncertainty. However, there are factors that help manifestation work.

Some people may find visualizing what they wish to manifest easier if they create a vision board. For instance, if they wish to manifest a new home, they look for pictures of a home that looks similar to what they want, cut or print them out, and then stick them on a board, perhaps with a title such as "My New Home for Next Year."

It is also important to be careful to focus on what you really want and be specific about the details. So say you are manifesting a new relationship. You need to decide whether having a partner who is loving and fun is more important than their physical appearance or whether both are equally important. Keep in mind that the more qualities you ask for, the longer the universe may take to respond.

Probably the biggest obstacle to manifestation is negative thinking, which cancels out the manifestation. For example, if you are focusing on manifesting a new job and a little later have the thought, *I'm not going to find a job*, the universe gets confused and in effect one thought cancels out the other. And if the negative thought is repeated enough times, then that is what the universe will provide. It is very easy to automatically create negative thoughts, such as *I am not worthy*, so keep a thought diary while you're manifesting to identify and correct the thoughts so they do not sabotage your manifestation.

To create a stronger manifestation, one or more people can add their energy together. They just need to be careful that they all focus on exactly the same manifestation because even small differences can confuse the universe as to what it is they all really want.

Another aspect of manifesting is to be sure your emotional energy is as positive as possible when you're doing the manifestation. This will ensure a higher vibration and thus a quicker response from the universe. It is like two checkout lines in a store—one long and one short. The long line is characterized by the lower vibration of the old consciousness and will take a while to move through. The shorter line is characterized by the higher vibration of the New Consciousness and will move along quickly. To be in a higher vibration, try to be in a state of joy or gratitude and avoid manifesting at a time when you are experiencing a negative emotion.

Finally, to raise the vibration of your manifestation, remember to thank the universe for making it happen and have patience while you are waiting for it to appear.

✧ Exercise: Manifesting

1. Write out your key desires in a new section of your journal.
2. Find time to sit with an open heart and be in a state of gratitude and positive emotion.
3. Say the manifestation and set the intention to let it go into the universe.
4. Thank the universe for making it happen and surrender to the process of creation.
5. There is no need to repeat the manifestation, but to strengthen it, you could imagine the positive emotions you will feel or how your life will change when your manifestation happens. And have patience.

When you manifest from a soul consciousness and not an ego consciousness there will be an alignment and harmony with the universe.

IN BALANCE WITH NATURE

Interacting and being in the presence of nature allows us to be in a state of mindfulness and gratitude for the gift it gives us. Growing our own food is one way to do this that also provides sustenance that is not contaminated with modern pesticides and has a high vibrational energy. We all live in different circumstances and how able we are to do this will vary depending on whether we are living in a city apartment and gardening in pots or out in the country and farming on an ample amount of land. However, the principles are the same.

Being in harmony with what we grow also enables us to be aware of nature. This can include factors such as knowing the amount of water available in the different seasons, paying attention to the cycle of planting and harvesting, and managing diseases and pests organically. All these things need to be learned, and in fact we can never stop learning!

Try talking to the plants and be aware that the love you give them will be absorbed as energy to be released again when consumed. Also, nature spirits in the land can be asked to help to encourage pests to be less troublesome.

Many years ago, Andy took a trip up the Amazon to visit some of the Indigenous tribes. At one point he met a seventy-year-old Colombian lady who had over sixty different plants in her garden that she used for herbal remedies. And people came long distances to be treated by her. As she did not speak the local language and had first come to the area as a young woman, Andy wondered where she had gotten the plant knowledge. Through an interpreter she told him that she talked to the plants and asked them what healing properties they had.

Andy's experience is consistent with the fact that everything—humans, animals, insects, and even the rocks and crystals of the Earth—has a consciousness that can be energetically communicated with. In our Pioneering New Consciousness workshop, we help students to learn how to do this because it is easier to do in the high vibration of the workshop. However, it is something everyone can eventually do if they have an open mind and develop their intuition.

Another tip is to create an area of high-energy vibration in the growing area. This means that everything grown there will have a high vibrational energy, and when the food is consumed, the high vibrational energy will be absorbed along with it.

✧ Exercise: Creating a High Vibration Area

This can be used for your home as well as your garden. It consists of a base crystal feeding energy to various other crystals in a boundary around the area.

1. You will need at least five crystals, a larger one for the base crystal and at least four smaller ones. The type of crystal is not that important, and quartz crystals are fine. You can also use your intuition or a pendulum to pick the crystals to make it more fun.

2. Hold the base crystal and set the intention to link it to two different high-energy centers at an energy level that is in the greatest interest of the land. These can be local energy centers that you know of or major Earth chakras. Living in Wiltshire in the UK, we use Glastonbury and Stonehenge.

3. Now hold the base crystal and the other crystals together and set the intention for the base crystal to be linked to the other crystals.

4. The base crystal, being larger, can be placed in a central position in full view, and the other crystals can be placed along the boundary of the area, either visible or not.

5. The whole area between the base and outside crystals is now an area of high vibration. There is no need to reinforce the energy links unless the energies get disturbed for some reason.

INNER PEACE

Inner peace helps moving to the New Consciousness, but it is not the absence of conflict from life, but the ability to cope with it.

The whole world is filled with negativity, which is mostly what we read about in the newspapers, see on television, or hear from someone else. But we have a choice as to how much of this negativity we absorb. Absorbing less, of course, will help us to gain inner peace. You may be amazed to find that you can disconnect from mainstream sources and their negativity and manipulation completely and still be aware of what's going on in the world from other sources. These tend to be smaller organizations or individuals using email or internet communication.

Another path to inner peace is being careful not to judge others. Unless we have all the information about a person or an event, it is best to avoid judgment. For example, if someone runs up and grabs an old man and pushes him into the wall of a building, is he trying to rob him or is he holding the old man against the wall to prevent a falling object from hitting him?

Judging is something that we do automatically, and as with any other habit, we can stop it through repeated and sustained practice. It may be helpful to keep in mind that the reason other people are in certain situations or become perpetrators may be part of their soul plan, and it's not our place to judge whether what is happening to them is good or bad, right or wrong. We can selectively choose to see the beauty in everything and focus on other people's strengths rather than their weaknesses.

We can try adopting the practice of knowing that the only person we can change is ourselves. If our intention is strong and comes from the deepest part of us, change will happen, and peace will come from making those changes.

Forgiveness also leads to inner peace. When we forgive, it allows us to see only the love in others and ourselves. Daily meditation during which we feel the unconditional love of something greater than ourselves may help.

Emotions dip and peak in line with how much control we have

over our own happiness. Inner peace comes when we can cope with all the conflicts in life and don't react to others' dramas.

Because our thoughts come and go unchallenged, most of us struggle through life unconsciously, accepting that we are our thoughts. We simply do not look at or challenge them as they appear and disappear. By accepting the thoughts—which are often about the past or the future—without examining them, we give them permission to shape our beliefs about ourselves and our lives. The only way these thoughts can hurt us is if we keep thinking about past experiences or worrying about future events, thereby bringing them into the present moment. We are not our thoughts about the past or the future, so fix your attention on the present moment as often as possible.

We gain inner peace not by trying to control the outer world but by gaining control of our inner world. When our thoughts reflect peace, those thoughts will extend outward, and a peaceful perception of the world will arise.

SUMMARY OF CHAPTER II

In the old consciousness we identified with our negative emotions and thoughts and hence attracted realities that matched this energy. The internal conflict drains the vital energy of our supreme life force and when we are depleted, we are not able to achieve Oneness or the New Consciousness.

Our lives in the past have been built around judgment and duality. We have moved away from the natural world into mental constructs based on judgment. As a result, we are unfulfilled and suffer mentally, emotionally, physically, and behaviorally. So our social and political world mirrors the same level of chaos. When we reach the New Consciousness, we will be able to look within and outside of ourselves without judgment. We will then be ready to start manifesting and creating a New Earth.

As within, so without.

CONCLUSION TO PART TWO

From a Galactic Being of Light:

From a Galactic perspective, Earth has more energy coming in now than it has ever experienced before to see if all are able to live in that high vibration state. Most of the other planets in the system have done this, but some have not passed and are staying with their current vibration. Contrary to popular belief, it is not necessary for Earth or its inhabitants to shift in order to enable this massive shift that the Galactic Council is moving toward. Because if it does not shift it will just be left behind.

Earth, bless Her, is trying to shift, but it is humans who are making it difficult for her to go. At some point she will make the decision to shake off the laggers and just go with the ones who are prepared. And that is what the Council is helping Earth to do. Because ultimately all souls that leave their physical vessels will end up going to different planets and launch pads. So, it really does not matter. So little of what your inhabitants think matters.

More and more downloads of energy are coming to the Earth, and how this energy will be used is dependent on the human inhabitants of Earth. They are very anchored and rooted in the extreme fear that has been on Earth for so long and in the ego and being in the head, with the ability to think but with little knowledge. It is very difficult to puncture through this so we just leave it to the energies.

If people are in extreme discomfort, they will be able to uproot themselves from the sludge and quicksand of fear and try to do something for themselves, but there is so much mud of helplessness. So, it is ignorance, ego, and helplessness that are the prevailing symptoms preventing their shift of consciousness. It is a cage that will stop them moving forward.

Earth has begun its shift to the New Consciousness, and an increasing number of souls are choosing to expand their consciousness and move to it. This is the process of moving from a fear-based environment to a love-based one. Currently everything appears rather chaotic, but it is the process of purification before the renewal.

This awakening happens differently for everyone. For some it can be a slow and steady process, while for others it can be a spontaneous one. It is completely beautiful and magical to experience the Oneness that a soul connection brings.

The road to expanding our consciousness is generally bumpy, full of thick mud pits and many roadblocks. To make it worse, modern life causes us to separate more from our soul and look for external answers to problems. In doing this, it frequently ignores or denies the root causes of our personal issues. We expect quick fixes, rather than real long-term changes.

It seems that over the last few decades people have been existing rather than living. Many try to run away or numb themselves rather than resolving their deepest issues and expanding their consciousness.

People who are starting to awaken can often feel entirely disconnected from those around them, as if peeling away from old lives. It is a beautiful, confusing, and painful time all at once. Expanding our consciousness forces us to move away from the external and connect more to the internal.

This is one of the hardest parts of awakening. How to break away from external temptations, values that our social groups share, belief systems, and cultural conditioning. However, the end result will make it all worthwhile.

When we expand our consciousness and find balance between our soul and the external world, we increase our confidence, integrity, and the conviction of our beliefs without the fear of being and expressing our true selves.

In a world of duality, there exists an inclination to view events, behaviors, and feelings with judgment: right or wrong, worthy or unworthy, valuable or invaluable, good or bad. Dualism leads to imbalance and fear, as we misunderstand the nature of seemingly opposite qualities. A balanced union between our soul and ego can unite, heal, and create anything. Synergy created by this union catalyzes the forces of creation into manifestation.

This book is intended to provide hope for a new future as we move into the New Earth. The light of Oneness is a reflection of the divine of life, and we are all a direct expression of this Oneness. This is not experienced through the fragmented vision of ego consciousness but in the expanded consciousness.

Unconditional love involves loving ourselves unconditionally first. Then it is simple to start unconditionally loving others. When we illuminate, acknowledge, accept, and integrate our shadow selves, we can have the strength of heart and mind to accept the shadow selves of others.

Within our society there seems to be so much pressure to conform to external ideals of perfection that to love ourselves has become a hard task to achieve. By acknowledging our shadow parts and loving ourselves, we break this unhealthy pattern of needing to be perfect according to society's standards. Then we can move on to unconditionally loving others as well. We can care about another person's happiness without demanding any benefits for ourselves. Unconditional love also means accepting other people for who they are, both their shadow and light selves.

Working through the exercises in the book will help you to expand your consciousness while moving through the journey to reach the next level of ascension mastery. This is possible for anyone because we have all the resources needed within. You have the choice to be steadfast in your new vision of life or to hold on to the comforts of the old consciousness.

Pay attention to your thoughts, feelings, words, and actions. Now is the time to become the master of your vibrational energy field. Everything has an effect on your vibration. You can choose what you are allowing into your energy field—thoughts and emotions that may be generated by you or by mainstream media or others.

Be aware that the New Consciousness is a blank canvas upon which you can begin to create a new world. To stay in your heart, stay neutral, take responsibility for your actions, act with honesty and integrity, and most of all maintain a balance with Mother Earth. You are the captain of your ship.

Through near-death experiences and between lives spiritual regression we can see the positive impact of expanding our consciousness. How much more amazing would it be if we could live our lives with an expanded consciousness to create a Golden Age.

In the final words of the Council of Beings of Light:

You are an expression and extension of Source. Simply allow it. We are holding the vision of the divine New Earth with you and from our vantage point it is glorious. We are with you every step of the way. You are loved beyond measure. We are with you . . . always. We love you.

Acknowledgments

We are grateful to Triona Sheeran, Anita Das, and Ioana-Cristiana Scumpu for contributing to the book and for the near-death experience case studies from the *Journal of Near-Death Studies*, the case studies from the Scientific and Medical Network, Pim van Lommel, and other contributors.

Thanks are extended to the clients and therapists of the Spiritual Regression Therapy Association who have enabled the between lives spiritual regression research to be completed, to those who shared their near-death experiences and stories, and to the authors and publishers who have enabled us to provide this information. Also, to Ian Lawton for his research work and ideas for *Exploring the Eternal Soul*, which have been used in this book.

And much gratitude goes to the spirits of light who have provided inspirational channeling and help in writing the book. These include the Council of Beings of Light, the Galactic Beings of Light, the Creators of Oneness, the Elders, and the Divine Mother.

Between Lives Spiritual Regression Therapy Research

The Past Life Regression Academy (PLRA)[1] was created in 2002, and the syllabus for its training was finalized at the first World Congress for Regression Therapy in 2006. Training programs in hypnosis, regression therapy, and between lives spiritual regression have been delivered in the UK since 2002, Norway since 2005, Turkey since 2007, Sweden and Singapore since 2008, India since 2010, Italy and South Africa since 2012, Mexico and Australia since 2013, the United States and Romania since 2015, and France since 2016. Over six hundred therapists have graduated from the training program in the nearly twenty years of its existence and have become past life therapists, regression therapists, and/or between lives spiritual regression (BLSR) therapists.

The BLSR therapists need to submit five case studies for final certification. The case studies are prepared to a standardized template that requires information to be provided in each of the categories listed below and what the client gains from each session.

+ Client name or number
+ Date of regression

- Client's prior hypnosis experience, rapport level, and cast of characters
- Hypnosis induction methods used
- Past life summary and death scene
- Crossing over
- Orientation stops
- Soul group
- Meeting the Wise Ones/Elders
- Next life selection
- Reincarnation
- Eternal Now
- Other spirit world activities
- The client's receptivity
- What made this session unique
- What the client gained from the session
- What I learned

As discussed in chapter 5, the information gained from the training of BLSR therapists provided 537 case studies from 108 therapists, which gave us a comprehensive database to work with. The PLRA training provided the structure and consistency for this research in the following ways:

- Each client had a pre-regression screening session to ensure they could enter deep hypnosis. The depth of hypnosis trance is important, as the person's conscious mind needs to be inactive. Various measurements can be used, including physical indicators, response time, and the volume of the voice when the client answers questions.
- Any personal issues that could affect entering the between life experience were cleared. This included past and current life personal issues or blockages.

+ To prevent leading the client, only open questions were used, such as, "Describe what you are aware of around you" and "What is being communicated to you?" Closed questions were confined to confirming information. Most of the time, commands were simple; for instance, "What happens next?" and "Tell me more."

+ Under deep hypnosis clients tend to take instructions extremely literally. This means that deliberate fabrication of information was nearly impossible, unless the person was not really in trance, and that is something that the PLRA therapist would have been able to detect. For the same reason, people could not just be told to experience something because for the most part they have to be actually having the experience to report on it.

METHODOLOGY

We went through the 537 BLSR cases and looked for factors within them that were similar to near-death experiences (NDEs). As we mentioned earlier, a major obvious difference between the BLSR and NDE experiences is that the BLSR was guided while the NDE evolved spontaneously. So, for example, therapists started the regression from a client's last past life and ensured that the heart had stopped before continuing. Thus, 100 percent of clients knew that they were dead in that last past life. Because NDE subjects had to return to the body, only the following five stages of the between lives spiritual regression could be used for comparison in the study:

1. Out of body/transition via a tunnel or light
2. Meeting with friends, family, or spirit guides
3. Varied perception of surroundings

4. Initial rest and energy restoring
5. Past life review (possibly through replay/role-play via life books and films)

To bring together the work of the NDE pioneers, we developed the table of common occurrences, shown on page 176, during an NDE. Our table is based on the work of van Lommel and the elements of his classification. We then added a couple of extra items to accommodate some of Greyson's research.

The numbers in the table denote the percentage of people that the researchers have reported to have had experienced that respective factor. For researchers who identified the corresponding factor but did not identify the percentage of people experiencing the different aspects, an X has been used instead of a number.

In comparing the NDE research data a number of factors need to be considered. Primarily, that the early pioneers doing the research worked quite independently of each other, so their definition of what constituted an NDE and the types of questions used to understand it varied. Also, many people cannot put the NDE into words, so they use metaphors that cannot be taken literally, and cultural background also affects the NDE experience. So, the questions asked to understand the experience need to take this into account.

Stage	Ring[2] (1980)	NDE Gallup[3] (1982)	NDE Greyson[4] (1983)	NDE Lommel[5] (2001)	NDE Fenwick[6] (1996)	BLSR AT, RK (2023)
		% of subjects	% of 74 subjects	% of 62 subjects	% of 300 subjects	% of 537 cases
Out-of-body experience	X	26	53	24	65	99
Awareness of being dead	X		27	50		100
Visual perceptions	X	23	38	23	24	77
Audible sounds or voices	X	17	22		24	6
Positive emotions (e.g., peace)	X	32	77	56	31	30
Light phenomena	X	14	43		72	62
Moving through a tunnel or darkness	X	9	32	31	51	11
Communication with light or other beings	X	23	12	23		69
Another world or celestial landscape		32	58	29	24	45
Meeting with deceased persons			26	32	33	21
Life review	X	32	22	13	17	60
Precognition		6	16		13	3

ANALYSIS

From the results it is evident that there are statistical similarities, correlations, and corroboration between the elements experienced during the NDE and the BLSR. All twelve elements of the NDE correspond to the BLSR process. The differences are in the variance between some of the percentage figures.

There is a higher percentage of awareness of being out of the body (99 percent) and being dead (100 percent) with BLSR compared to NDE. This is because an NDE is spontaneous and unexpected, and the person is not always aware of what is happening. For a BLSR, therapists ensure the past life character's heart has stopped beating at the point of their past life death and that they have left the body by asking the client whether these events have occurred. Only 1 percent of BLSR clients went through the five main stages while still energetically connected to the body, before leaving the body at a later stage. Interesting, this 1 percent corresponds with Reena's NDE (described in the preface) where she had contact with the light beings and a life review before she had the out-of-body experience.

Unexpectedly, there are significantly fewer accounts of positive emotions in the BLSR accounts than the NDE accounts. Many NDE subjects experience joy, peace, being one with everything, and receiving unconditional love from a divine being. This is similar to when BLSR clients go through the healing stage, where the old emotions are stripped off, and only positive ones are left. However, only 30 percent of the BLSR accounts mention positive emotions. The reason for this may be because our therapists do not ask questions to ascertain emotions during these stages of the process. The positive emotions that were included were spontaneously reported.

With BLSR accounts, there was a much higher percentage of visual perception, light phenomena, and communication with light beings by the participants. With BLSR accounts our therapists are trained to ask the clients to describe the scene around them. So, there are plenty of light descriptions and visual perceptions. Also, many of the clients who have had BLSR sessions have read either Michael Newton's and/or Andy's books and are familiar with light beings. So while being regressed they will use this familiar language as it filters through their perceptions. While it is possible this familiarity may have biased the results, clients in very deep hypnosis answer questions literally without conscious mind involvement. We are unsure if the people who have had an NDE have had the same amount of familiarity with light beings and the corresponding language.

Surprisingly, there are significantly fewer BLSR accounts of moving through a tunnel or darkness than with NDEs. Many of the BLSR accounts report transitioning and moving through light. There are a multitude of varied descriptions of the transition (including a hand pulling them up, a glass elevator shaft, and a staircase of light, to name a few). But only 11 percent of the accounts reported moving through a tunnel or darkness.

The last area where there is a percentage variance is in the results for a life review. The BLSR accounts have a significantly higher number of life reviews than the NDE accounts. A possible reason for this is that those who experience the NDE are turned back before their life review because the information may affect free will in completing their current life soul plan. BLSR clients are screened to be open to this learning should it emerge. The number may have been even higher except that in some BLSR accounts, the past life review happened at a later point in the cycle and so was not included in the count.

When the past life review took place in a BLSR, it was in great detail, and some clients had auditory experiences and some visual experiences. The NDE life reviews, when they happened, were similar to BLSR past life reviews in giving deeper insights, often with advice from spiritual beings.[7]

Those who have experienced an NDE report that time appears to be nonexistent, with everything happening all at once. This has similarities with BLSR afterlife experiences.[8]

SUMMARY

Despite the differences in the percentages, this new research has shown that there is strong correlation and corroboration between BLSR and NDE accounts. The strength of the PLRA research comes from the 537 BLSR cases from people around the world that were collected over fifteen years.

APPENDIX 2

Past Life Regression Research

Past life regression is a technique that uses hypnosis to recover memories of past lives or incarnations. It is typically undertaken in a psychotherapeutic setting to resolve trauma or related difficulties in the current life. The first step of guiding clients into past lives is to allow them to go into a deep state of relaxation—also known as hypnosis. In this state of focused attention, the client can access the deeper aspects of consciousness a lot more easily than in the normal state.

Those being guided into a hypnotic state are asked to close their eyes and make themselves comfortable. Then, using a hypnotic voice and certain words, the therapist helps them to go into a state of mental and physical relaxation. Clients are guided back and encouraged to contact a past life related to the problem they have.

This appendix will focus on Reena's past life regression research, which resulted in the three books in the Radiant Light series. The methodology or parts of it that she established may be of use to others doing this type of research. Careful nonleading questioning and diligent research are important parts of this work.

SELECTION OF SUBJECTS

Over a four-year period, eight clients coming to Reena for entirely different reasons spontaneously recalled events in a past life related to the life and times of Jesus. The eight clients were unknown to each other and from different parts of the world. Subsequent sessions with each of them revealed more information, and it was from this information that the research was done.

METHODOLOGY

The sessions were not conducted so much for therapeutic reasons but for information gathering. So the method used to collect details was slightly different from those used in therapeutic sessions. The subjects were still in a hypnotic state, but a refined way of gathering information was used to ensure that the subject remained in the experience and their conscious mind was not engaged.

An example of this is gathering names. For therapy, the main thread that is followed is concerned with emotional issues. The name of the past life character is not required, as it does not affect the therapeutic experience of the client. Only when the name comes up spontaneously is a note made for future reference if needed.

However, in the case of this research it was important to get information like dates and names of people and places for the purposes of research and cross-referencing to verify the validity of the stories that emerged. Unless fully embodied in the experience, just asking the subject under hypnosis, "What is your name?" will often take the person out of the experience and into their conscious mind. This is not ideal as they may access the information from books or the internet as opposed to the experience.

What Reena did predominantly when the subject was at a relevant point of the story was to ask, "How are you addressed?" This kept the subject in the experience of the memory and got a more authentic response. However, this created another problem because the subject might not have used an actual name. For example, Jesus was addressed as teacher, son, brother, father, or husband or by a respective nickname given to him by certain people. The way Reena overcame this was to ask the person at multiple significant points in their regression, "How are you addressed?" and use the majority rules principle to then determine the name.

Age was another difficult detail to obtain. Even in our current life, when asked about a past memory we normally remember the experience, but we get slightly fuzzy about the age we were when it happened. The same principle applies to past life recollection. For this Reena asked questions like, "At what point of your life does this occur?" and "Are you a child, a teenager, an adult, or an elderly person?" then tried as much as possible to home in on a reasonably small age range. Of course, if the age came spontaneously, then it was used.

The most authentic past life experiences elicit deep emotional responses. For example, most people who were regressed and witnessed the torture of Jesus felt deep emotions and expressed them quite visually and audibly, either by crying, softening their voice, or staying silent as they tried to manage the emotions so they could speak. Experiencing deep emotions as a reaction to events is one of the ways to determine the authenticity of the experience.

If the past life experience is made up by the conscious mind, there will be little to no emotion displayed by the person. However, if they are experiencing a memory via the wider conscious mind then the emotions that they exhibit are deep, intense, and totally authentic. The same applies to positive emotions.

RESULTS

In the table below are the accounts of five subjects (identified by their name in the past life) with page references to their accounts as they are described in the book *Shrouded Truth*. These are James (the brother of Jesus), Mary Magdalene, Marta (sister of Mary Magdalene), Thomas, and Sara Tamar (daughter of Mary Magdalene).

ACCOUNT	JAMES	MARY	MARTA	THOMAS	SARA TAMAR
Jesus had children with his wife Mary Magdalene	30, 39	133, 150	187	207–208	220, 240
Mary Magdalene was not a prostitute but Jesus's chief apostle		146–163	171–174		243
Jesus and Mary lived in France	29, 37	146–159			241–244

Jesus Had Children with His Wife Mary Magdalene

There are indications in Gnosticism that Jesus and Mary Magdalene shared an amorous relationship. The Gnostic Gospel of Philip tells that Jesus "kissed her often" and refers to Mary as his "companion." Several sources from the thirteenth century claim that an aspect of Cathar theology was the belief that the earthly Jesus had a familial relationship with Mary Magdalene.[1] Historical annals also hypothesize that in September 33 CE, a daughter was born to Mary Magdalene.

Mary Magdalene Was Not a Prostitute but Jesus's Chief Apostle

The Church denounced Mary Magdalene, even going as far as calling her a prostitute. Laurence Gardner's hypothesis is that the succession via apostolic constitution is the reason why the Church began to denounce any women who were closely involved in the ministry of Jesus. They wanted to denounce any form of family hereditary claims to the succession of the Church, thereby strengthening the apostolic succession through followers dating back to Peter and Paul.[2]

This was taken further in the third century, when a process of segregation had commenced in churches led by the Romans, where men performed the rites and women worshipped in silence. And in 1977, Pope Paul VI, the same pope who in 1969 had released the revised Church doctrine stating that Mary Magdalene was no longer considered a prostitute, reaffirmed that a woman could not become a priest.[3] In doing so, the Church relegated women to the level of second-class citizens, which was contrary to the equal place they were given within the Nazarene community and within Jesus's ministry.

Jesus and Mary Lived in France

Of all the branches of Christian belief, only the Cathars ever accepted that Jesus and Mary Magdalene were married. This was probably because their ancestors living in France in the first century had met Mary and Jesus as a couple and, undisturbed for centuries, these beliefs were then passed down from father to son or from mother to daughter for hundreds of years.[4]

In the twelfth-century *Chronica Majora* of Matthew Paris, it was confirmed that Mary Magdalene died at La Sainte-Baume in

63 CE,[5] in the Provence-Alpes-Côte d'Azur region of southeastern France. It lies twenty-five miles east of Aix-en-Provence. The grotto of Mary Magdalene is a Christian pilgrimage site to this day, and her relics, including her skull, found in 1279, are held within her tomb in Saint Maximin la Sainte-Baume, which has been described as one of the most precious relics in all Christendom[6] and declared as Christianity's third most important tomb by the Vatican.[7]

APPENDIX 3

New Consciousness Workshops and Therapy Associations

Additional resources are available for those moving to the New Consciousness. This includes residential workshops that have overnight accommodation, home study courses, and some therapy associations that we can recommend.

THE AUTHORS' WEBSITES

Both Reena Kumarasingham and Andy Tomlinson have information about moving into the New Consciousness and energy therapy on their websites.
reenakumarasingham.com
andy-tomlinson.com

PIONEERING THE NEW CONSCIOUSNESS USING ADVANCED VIBRATIONAL TECHNIQUES

These residential workshops are led by Reena and Andy and supervised by the Council of Beings of Light through intuitive direction and interactive channeling. It allows those attending to experience being in the high vibrations of the New Consciousness. The Council of Beings of Light have shared techniques for living and working in the New Consciousness. These are effective methods for using energies in a powerful, harmonic way in this new dimension. This intensive seven-day training is highly practical and includes lectures, interactive discussions, demonstrations, and practice sessions.

pioneeringnewconsciousness.com

EMPOWERING THE DIVINE FEMININE

This home study course has been developed by Reena to empower the Divine Feminine within, so you can shine like the radiant being you are. It covers eleven topics leading to a major mind shift: moving away from polarizing male and female energy toward harmonizing critical aspects within ourselves to achieve Oneness.

reenakumarasingham.com

EMBODYING THE DIVINE CONSCIOUSNESS

This home study course was also developed by Reena to enable us to anchor to our own internal divine consciousness. This enables us to move through this change of consciousness with stability, clarity, and peace. It covers eleven topics leading to a major mind shift and helping you to disengage from the external world and engage more with your internal world.

reenakumarasingham.com

BETWEEN LIVES SPIRITUAL
REGRESSION TRAINING

The Past Life Regression Academy offers home study between lives spiritual regression training for therapists trained in hypnosis and regression therapy. Enjoy the classroom training from the comfort of your own home, at your own pace.

reenakumarasingham.com

SPIRITUAL REGRESSION
THERAPY ASSOCIATION

This is an international association of regression therapists and between lives spiritual regression therapists that respect the spiritual nature of their clients. They are professionally trained to international standards and work according to a code of ethics that respects the clients' welfare. **regressionassociation.com**

EARTH ASSOCIATION OF
REGRESSION THERAPY

This is an independent association with the objective to improve and enlarge the professional application of regression therapy. It provides internet forums, newsletters, and professional standards for the regression therapy training schools that it recognizes. Every summer it offers a series of workshops for ongoing professional development. **earthassociation.org**

Glossary

astral plane: The dimension closely linked to the physical world, which the spiritual body normally passes through and in which trapped spirits reside.

between lives spiritual regression: The experience of soul memories between lives in the spirit plane during deep hypnosis. This is also known as the interlife, between lives or Life Between Lives.

chakra: There are seven major energy centers in the body from the crown chakra on the top of the head to the base chakra at the base of the body that help with the circulation of energy around the body.

Cocreators of the Oneness: Spirits of light creating different conscious realities and life forms on various planets. Currently they are helping Earth create the New Consciousness.

consciousness: An awareness of what we experience with our senses, the positive and negative emotions of life, and the experiences of images, ideas, words, and thoughts as, for example, we read a novel or remember the past. However, near-death experiences and between lives spiritual regressions suggest that our consciousness is also outside of the physical body and continues after death.

Council of Beings of Light: Spirits of light directing the change of consciousness on Earth who have navigated this change on their own planets before.

Divine Mother: The soul consciousness of Earth sometimes called Gaia.

Elders: The wise and experienced souls who assist those still incarnating with a past life review and next-life planning advice. They work at a different level from spirit guides. Clients call them a variety of names, such as Wise Ones, Higher Ones, Masters, or Council.

emotional lessons: An emotion that a soul is attempting to master by experiencing it in a physical form on Earth. Members of the same soul group often work on the same lesson together.

expanded consciousness: Having a wider spiritual perspective that includes past lives, near-death experiences, and the existence of our eternal soul.

fluidity: Between lives sessions vary in their order of events, how extensively any event is experienced, and also in frequency, such as the number of visits to see the Elders.

Galactic Beings of Light: Spirits of light who work with the Council of Beings of Light to direct the change of consciousness on different planets in the galaxy.

gratitude: Appreciation of what we have and a way of raising our energy vibration.

grounding: Discharging any surplus energy to Earth and bringing our focus back to the body.

inner peace: An ability to cope with whatever conflict happens in life.

intuition: Our first instinct that we feel or sense before the analytical mind becomes involved.

life path: The most probable course of a life if that person makes the decisions that they planned in the spirit plane. The soul may also have agreed to certain triggers that are intended to prompt them to stay on that path.

life preview: A foretaste of the next life that is received in the spirit plane and represents the major probabilities for the upcoming life.

lucid dreaming: Vivid dreams that the dreamer can control to some extent.

manifesting: Requesting our desires from the universe.

medium: Someone who has developed their psychic abilities to be able to communicate with deceased people. This differs from a clairvoyant, who has psychic abilities to communicate with evolved spirits of light such as the Elders.

mindfulness: Focusing on the present using our five physical senses to experience everything about the moment we are in.

near-death experience: A set of spiritual events that are experienced when a person comes very close to dying, the memory of which stays with them when they survive. People can have various experiences during this period, but it is often a significant turning point in their lives that can lead to a major life change.

New Consciousness: A different vibrational energy that the Earth is moving toward and humans can choose to be part of. They will move from a world of fear and greed to one of love, joy, and harmony with nature.

next-life planning: The whole process of life-planning discussions with Elders, spirit guides, and soul mates.

Oneness: A state of being associated with Source or God and everything.

out-of-body experience: This is the sense of having separated from the physical body and of viewing it from the outside. This happens spontaneously during near-death experiences, in a life-threatening situation, or by conscious intent.

past life: A previous life experienced as part of the reincarnation cycle.

past life review: The process of reviewing and learning from the last life in the between lives. It involves an element of discussion with Elders, spirit guides, and soul mates.

regression: The process for a client to enter into an altered state of awareness so that they can recall a past life or between lives memories. This is usually achieved by hypnosis, but other methods can be used.

savant syndrome: A rare condition of people with a developmental disorder who have an astonishing ability or brilliance that stands in marked contrast to their overall limitations.

shadow self: An archetype of the unconscious mind composed of cultural conditioning, repressed ideas, instincts, impulses, weaknesses, desires, and embarrassing fears.

soul: The spiritual consciousness that contains all of a person's past life experiences and learning.

soul consciousness: A wise, unconditionally loving, creative wholeness that represents our most authentic state of being.

soul groups: Groups of soul mates that work closely together both in the spirit plane and in successions of lives in the physical realm.

Source: The ultimate source of everything, the creator of the universe, and what our individual soul consciousness is connected to. Sometimes it's called the Oneness; various religions have other names.

spirit attachment: The consciousness of a person that survives death but does not go to the spirit plane for some reason and instead attaches itself to another person's energy field.

spirit guides: Specialist souls who oversee the life plan of those who are incarnate. They provide guidance and advice when asked and during the past life review and next-life planning.

spirit plane: The true home of all soul energies and the realm most closely connected with Source itself. Sometimes it is called the spirit realm.

spirits of light: A general term for any soul in the spirit realm.

synchronicity: A way in which the universe communicates helpful information through timely yet unexpected events.

telepathy: An ability to transmit information by the power of thought to another person anywhere in the world.

terminal lucidity: When a person becomes completely lucid for hours or days before they die even though the brain is not working or is damaged.

veil of amnesia: The process by which a reincarnating soul gradually loses its memory of the spirit plane and the life planning that has taken place. The aim is to prevent us from feeling homesick and from taking a "life exam" knowing all the answers in advance. It may not be completely in place until early childhood.

Notes

CHAPTER 1. CONSCIOUSNESS

1. Encyclopedia Britannica Online, s.v. "Wolfgang-Amadeus-Mozart."
2. J. David Sweatt, "Studies of Human Learning and Memory," in *Mechanisms of Memory*, 2nd ed. (Academic Press, 2010).
3. "Stephen Wiltshire's London Panorama," Stephen Wiltshire's website.
4. K. Konkoly et al., "Real-Time Dialogue between Experimenters and Dreamers during REM Sleep," *Current Biology* 31 (April 12, 2021): 1–11.
5. U. Voss et al., "Lucid Dreaming: A State of Consciousness with Features of Both Waking and Non-Lucid Dreaming," *Sleep* 32, no. 9 (2009): 1191–200.
6. M. Ullman, S. Krippner, and A. Vaughan, *Dream Telepathy: Experiments in Nocturnal E.S.P.*, 3rd ed. (Charlottesville, VA: Hampton Roads, 2002).
7. S. J. Sherwood and C. A. Roe, "A Review of Dream ESP Studies Conducted Since the Maimonides Dream ESP Programme," *Journal of Consciousness Studies* 10 (2003): 88.
8. G. E. R. Schwartz, "Accuracy and Replicability of Anomalous After-Death Communication Across Highly Skilled Mediums," *Journal of the Society for Psychical Research* 65, no. 1 (2001): 1–25.
9. D. J. Bem, "Review of G. E. Schwartz's The Afterlife Experiments: Breakthrough Scientific Evidence of Life after Death," *Journal of Parapsychology* 69 (2005): 173–83.
10. A. Delorme et al., "Electrocortical Activity Associated with Subjective Communication with the Deceased," *Frontiers in Psychology* 4 (2013): 834.
11. R. Monroe, *Journeys Out of the Body* (Garden City, NY: Doubleday, 1971).
12. M. D. Mumford, A. M. Rose, and D. A. Goslin, *An Evaluation of Remote Viewing: Research and Applications*, American Institutes for Research, 1995.
13. S. Blackmore, "A Postal Survey of OBEs," *Journal of the Society for Psychical Research* 52, no. 796 (1984): 225–44.
14. Wikipedia, s.v. "Emanuel Swedenborg."

15. S. Muldoon and H. Carrington, *Projection of the Astral Body* (London: Rider, 1929).

16. P. van Lommel, *Consciousness Beyond Life: The Science of the Near-Death Experience* (New York: HarperCollins, 2010), 41–42.

17. Nahm, M. et al., "Terminal Lucidity: A Review and a Case Collection," *Archives of Gerontology and Geriatrics* 55, no. 1 (July–August 2012): 138–42.

18. S. Haig, "The Brain: The Power of Hope," *Time*, January 29, 2007.

19. S. Brayne, H. Lovelace, and P. Fenwick, "End-of-Life Experiences and the Dying Process in a Gloucestershire Nursing Home as Reported by Nurses and Care Assistants," *American Journal of Hospice and Palliative Care* 25 (2008): 195–206.

20. E. Walker, *The Physics of Consciousness* (New York: Perseus Books, 2000), 152.

CHAPTER 2. NEAR-DEATH EXPERIENCES

1. K. Ring, "Amazing Grace: The Near-Death Experience as a Compensatory Gift," *Journal of Near-Death Studies* 10, no. 1 (1991): 25–27.

2. G. Gallup and W. Proctor, *Adventures in Immortality: A Look beyond the Threshold of Death* (New York: McGraw-Hill, 1982).

3. K. Ring, *Life at Death: A Scientific Investigation of the Near-Death Experience* (New York: Coward, McCann & Geoghegan, 1980), 32–37.

4. M. Sabom, *Recollections of Death: An Investigation Revealing Striking New Medical Evidence of Life after Death* (London: Corgi, 1982), 82.

5. K. Ring and S. Cooper, *Mindsight: Near-Death and Out-of-Body Experiences in the Blind*, 2nd ed. (Bloomington, IN: iUniverse, 1999), 28, 43, 49.

6. M. Sabom, *Light and Death: One Doctor's Fascinating Account of Near-Death Experiences* (Grand Rapids, MI: Zondervan Publishing House, 1998).

7. P. van Lommel, "Near-Death Experience in Survivors of Cardiac Arrest: A Prospective Study in the Netherlands," *Lancet* 358, no. 9298 (2001): 2039–45.

8. Bruce Greyson, "What Do Near-Death Experiences Mean for the Next Life—and for This Life?" (lecture, Scientific and Medical Network, November 6, 2021).

9. K. Ring, "Amazing Grace," 16–17.

10. P. van Lommel, "Near-Death Experience," 2039–45.

11. B. Greyson, "Near Death Experiences and Attempted Suicide," *Suicide and Life Threatening Behavior* 11 (1981): 10–16.

12. H. Cassol et al., "Near-Death Experience Memories Include More Episodic Components Than Flashbulb Memories," *Frontiers in Psychology* 888 (2020), 1–11.

13. S. J. Blackmore and T. Troscianko, "The Physiology of the Tunnel," *Journal of Near-Death Studies* 8 (1988), 15–28.

14. O. Blanke et al., "Stimulating Illusory Own-Body Perceptions," *Nature* 419 (September 2002): 269.

15. S. Parnia, "Death and Consciousness: An Overview of the Mental and Cognitive Experience of Death," *Annals of the New York Academy of Sciences* 130 (2014): 75–93.

16. R. Moody with P. Perry, *The Light Beyond* (New York: Bantam, 1988), 136.

17. E. Alexander, *Proof of Heaven: A Neurosurgeon's Journey into the Afterlife* (Simon and Schuster, 2012), 39–41, 141–42.

CHAPTER 3. PAST LIVES

1. J. Tucker, *Return to Life: Extraordinary Cases of Children Who Remember Past Lives* (New York: St. Martin's Press, 2013), 88–102.

2. I. Stevenson, *Twenty Cases Suggestive of Reincarnation* (Charlottesville, VA: University of Virginia Press), 1974.

3. I. Stevenson, *Cases of the Reincarnation Type*, vol. 1, Ten Cases in India (Charlottesville, VA: University of Virginia, 1975).

4. J. Tucker, "I've Been Here Before: Children's Reports of Previous Lives," *Shift: At the Frontiers of Consciousness* 17 (2007): 14–19.

5. I. Stevenson, *Where Reincarnation and Biology Intersect* (Westport, CT: Praeger Publishers, 1997), 38–41.

6. A. Tomlinson, *Exploring the Eternal Soul: Insights from the Life between Lives*, 3rd ed. (Salisbury. From the Heart Press, 2012), 202–04.

7. I. Stevenson, *Reincarnation and Biology: A Contribution to the Etiology of Birthmarks and Birth Defects* (Westport, CT: Praeger Publishers, 1997).

8. J. Tucker, *Life before Life: A Scientific Investigation of Children's Memories of Previous Lives* (New York: St. Martin's Press, 2005).

9. J. Tucker, "A Scale to Measure the Strength and Weakness of Children's Claims of Previous Lives: Methodology and Initial Findings," *Journal of Scientific Exploration* 14, no. 4 (2000): 571–81.

10. J. B. Tucker, "Children's Reports of Past-Life Memories: A Review," *Explore* 4 (2008): 244–48.

11. P. Ramster, *The Truth about Reincarnation* (Adelaide, Australia: Rigby, 1980).

12. P. Ramster, *In Search of Lives Past* (Somerset, UK: Somerset Film and Publishing, 1992).

13. A. Tomlinson, "Past Life Regression," in U. James, *Clinical Hypnosis Textbook* (London: Radcliffe Publishing, 2010), 292–94.

14. R. Kumarasingham, *Shrouded Truth* (Salisbury, From the Heart Press, 2018).

15. I. Stevenson and S. Pasricha, "A Preliminary Report on an Unusual Case of the Reincarnation Type with Xenoglossy," *Journal of the American Society for Psychical Research* 74 (1980): 331–48.

16. This research is still underway and the pilot results were provided by team member Alfonso Crosetto, email: alfonso.crosetto@gmail.com.

CHAPTER 4. BETWEEN LIVES SPIRITUAL REGRESSION

1. A. Tomlinson, "A Spiritual Perspective of Life and Death," *Kindred Spirit* January/February (2016): 96–97.

2. E. Fiore, *You Have Been Here Before: A Psychologist Looks at Past Lives* (New York: Ballantine Books, 1979).

3. P. Ramster, *The Truth about Reincarnation* (Adelaide, Australia: Rigby, 1980).

4. J. Whitton and J. Fisher, *Life Between Life* (New York: Warner Books, 1988).

5. D. Cannon, *Between Death and Life: Conversations with a Spirit* (Huntsville, AR: Ozark Mountain Publishing, 2003).

6. S. Modi, *Remarkable Healings: A Psychiatrist Uncovers Unsuspected Roots of Mental and Physical Illness* (Newburyport, MA: Hampton Roads, 1997).

7. M. Newton, *Journey of Souls: Case Studies of Life between Lives* (Woodbury, MN: Llewellyn, 1994).

8. M. Newton, *Destiny of Souls: New Case Studies of Life between Lives* (Woodbury, MN: Llewellyn, 2000).

9. A. Tomlinson, *Exploring the Eternal Soul: Insights from Past Life and Spiritual Regression* (Salisbury, From the Heart Press, 2006).

10. A. Tomlinson, *Exploring the Eternal Soul*, 300.

11. A. Tomlinson, *Exploring the Eternal Soul*, 167.

12. A. Tomlinson, *Exploring the Eternal Soul*, 165–169.

CHAPTER 5. COMPARISON OF NEAR-DEATH EXPERIENCES AND BETWEEN LIVES SPIRITUAL REGRESSIONS

1. K. Ring, "Amazing Grace: The Near-Death Experience as a Compensatory Gift," *Journal of Near-Death Studies* 10, no. 1 (1991): 29–32.

2. E. Fenwick and P. Fenwick, *The Truth in the Light* (London: Headline, 1996)

3. P. Fenwick and E. Fenwick, *The Art of Dying* (London: Continuum, 2008).

4. Visit the Past Life Regression Academy website for more information.

5. You can find a list of therapists on the "Find a Therapist" page of the Spiritual Regression Therapy Association website.

6. A. Tomlinson, *Exploring the Eternal Soul: Insights from Past Life and Spiritual Regression* (Salisbury, From the Heart Press, 2006), 275.

7. N. Bush, *Dancing Past the Dark: Distressing Near-Death Experiences* (self-pub. 2012).

8. H. Cassol, et al., "A Systematic Analysis of Distressing Near-Death Experience Accounts," *Memory* 27, no. 8 (2019).

CONCLUSION TO PART ONE

1. D. J. Chalmers, "Facing Up to the Problem of Consciousness," *Journal of Consciousness Studies* 2, no. 3 (1995): 200–19.

CHAPTER 6. SHIFTING TO AN AWAKENING WORLD

1. Wikipedia, s.v. "axial precession."

2. Wikipedia, s.v. "particle duality."

3. D. Hawkins, *Power vs. Force* (Carlsbad, CA: Hay House, 1995).

4. "Water, Drinks, and Hydration," NHS (website).

5. B. Lipton, *The Biology of Belief* (Carlsbad, CA: Hay House, 2005).

6. S. C. Segerstrom and G. E. Miller, "Psychological Stress and the Human Immune System: A Meta-Analytic Study of 30 Years of Inquiry," *Psychological Bulletin* 130, no. 4 (2004): 601–30.

7. F. Shapiro, *Eye Movement Desensitizing and Reprocessing: Basic Principles, Protocols and Procedures*, 2nd ed. (New York: Guildford Press, 2001).

8. F. Friedberg, *Do-It-Yourself Eye Movement Technique for Emotional Healing* (Oakland, CA: New Harbinger Publications, 2001).
9. See the "Find a Therapist" page on the Spiritual Regression Therapy Association website.
10. Visit the Earth Association for Regression Therapy website.
11. "Rape Victim Meets Attacker to Forgive Him," January 9, 2014, BBC website.

CHAPTER 7. ENERGY MANAGEMENT

1. A. Tomlinson, ed., *Transforming the Eternal Soul: Further Insights from Regression Therapy*, 4th ed. (Salisbury, From the Heart Press, 2022), 177–230.
2. J. Cresswell et al., "Mindfulness Training and Physical Health: Mechanisms and Outcomes," *Psychosomatic Medicine* 81, no. 3 (April 2019); S. Goldberg et al., "Mindfulness-Based Interventions for Psychiatric Disorders: A Systematic Review and Meta-Analysis," *Clinical Psychology Review* 59 (February 2018).
3. "Alan Sanderson, M.D., M.R.C.P., M.R.C.Psych," "Authors" page on the Inner Traditions website.
4. A. Tomlinson, *Exploring the Eternal Soul: Insights from the Life between Lives*, 3rd ed. (Salisbury, From the Heart Press, 2018), 188–89.
5. See the list of spirit release therapists on the "Find a Therapist" page of the Spiritual Regression Therapy Association website.
6. See the Earth Association for Regression Therapy website.

CHAPTER 8. BOUNDARIES FOR THE NEW CONSCIOUSNESS

1. J. Dimsdale, "Brainwashing Has a Grim History That We Shouldn't Dismiss," *Psyche* (November 24, 2021).
2. Wikipedia, s.v. "Milgram experiment."

CHAPTER 9. LISTENING TO OUR SOUL CONSCIOUSNESS

1. "Non-Dominant Hand Writing Therapy," Psychologies website, March 17, 2022.

CHAPTER 10. DEEPENING THE CONNECTION WITH OUR SOUL CONSCIOUSNESS

1. "Ashtiaq Asghar Detained for Canal Murder in Rotherham," BBC News website, December 21, 2011.

CHAPTER 11. CREATING A NEW EARTH THROUGH OUR SOUL CONSCIOUSNESS

1. S. B. Breathnach, *Simple Abundance* (New York: Warner Books, 1995).
2. Robert Emmons, "What Is Gratitude and How Can We Foster It?" *The Do Gooders Podcast, Caring Magazine*, November 25, 2019.
3. D. Newman, A. Gordon, and W. Mendes, "Comparing Daily Physiological and Psychological Benefits of Gratitude and Optimism Using a Digital Platform," *Emotion* 21, no. 7 (October 2021): 1357–65.

APPENDIX 1. BETWEEN LIVES REGRESSION THERAPY RESEARCH

1. Visit the Past Life Regression Academy website for more information.
2. K. Ring, *Life at Death: A Scientific Investigation of the Near-Death Experience* (New York: Coward, McCann & Geoghegan, 1980), 32–37.
3. K. Ring, *Book Review of Adventures in Immortality: A Look beyond the Threshold of Death*, by G. Gallup and W. Proctor. University of North Texas Digital Library.
4. B. Greyson, "The Near-Death Experience Scale," *Journal of Nervous & Mental Disease* 171, no. 6 (June 1983).
5. P. van Lommel, "Near-Death Experience in Survivors of Cardiac Arrest: A Prospective Study in the Netherlands," *Lancet* 358, no. 9298 (2001): 2039–2045.
6. P. Fenwick and E. Fenwick, *The Truth in the Light* (London: Headline, 1996).
7. A. Tomlinson, *Healing the Eternal Soul: Insights from Past Life and Spiritual Regression* (Salisbury, From the Heart Press, 2005), 111–13.
8. A. Tomlinson, *Exploring the Eternal Soul: Insights from the Life between Lives*, 3rd. ed. (Salisbury, From the Heart Press, 2012), 275.

APPENDIX 2. PAST LIFE REGRESSION RESEARCH

1. Wikipedia, s.v. "Jesus bloodline"; V. Wineyard, "Mary Magdalene and the Cathars," *I Write about Mary Magdalene* (blog).

2. L. Gardner, *The Magdalene Legacy* (Newburyport, MA: Weiser Books, 2007), 160.

3. L. Gardner, *The Grail Enigma* (New York: Harper Element, 2009), 111–44.

4. V. Wineyard, "Mary Magdalene."

5. L. Gardner, *Magdalene Legacy*, 198.

6. Wikipedia, s.v. "Relics of Mary Magdalene."

7. Y. Bridonneau, *The Tomb of Mary Magdalene Saint Maximin la Sainte Baumeå: Christianity's Third Most Important Tomb* (Saint-Rémy-de-Provence, France: Edisud, 2006).

Index

About the Authors

Andy Tomlinson is a psychotherapist and the founder of the Past Life Regression Academy, established in 2002, that has trained more than six hundred past life, current life, and between lives spiritual regression therapists worldwide. He is a founding member of the Spiritual Regression Therapy Association and the Earth Association of Regression Therapy and has been the president of the Society of Medical Advance and Research with Regression Therapy. Andy has been coteaching Pioneering the New Consciousness workshops since 2014 using Advanced Vibration Techniques as well as teaching shorter workshops training healers to clear a wide range of intrusive energies.

He is the author of *Exploring the Eternal Soul* and *Healing the Eternal Soul* and the editor of *Transforming the Eternal Soul*.

Reena Kumarasingham has been a regression therapist, between life spiritual regression therapist, and a certified international trainer for the Past Life Regression Academy for ten years. She has trained therapists in the UK, Australia, Singapore, and the United States, specializing in between lives spiritual regression since

2014. She also developed this training for the internet classroom and home study. Reena has been teaching Advanced Vibrational Techniques in Pioneering New Consciousness workshops since 2014 to help people transition and live in the New Consciousness with calm, peace, and empowerment.

She is the author of the highly acclaimed Radiant Light series, comprising *Shrouded Truth, The Magdalene Lineage*, and *Divine Consciousness*.